# Contraduction

# Contraduction

## Dan Barker

# HYPATIA PRESS

Published by Hypatia Press in the United Kingdom in 2024

ISBN: 978-1-83919-597-6

Illustrations by Marcos Telias

www.hypatiapress.org

# Advance Praise

An ingenious word for an invaluable concept. Sharp, clear, and timely.

  – Steven Pinker, Johnstone Professor of Psychology, Harvard University, author of *The Blank Slate* and *Rationality*

To humans, any sufficiently advanced technology would appear as magic. Likewise, the "fine tuning" of our universe strikes many of us gullible primates as evidence for an intelligent, purposeful creator. In his engaging new book, Dan Barker deconstructs this fallacy with cool rationality and down-to-earth wit while introducing a useful new word to our lexicon.

  – Ron Reagan, commentator and broadcaster, son of former President Reagan

Both a delightful read and a penetrating argument: Barker has invented an invaluable new concept, and puts it to work with clarity, wit, and above all conclusiveness. A must-have book!

  – Philosopher A. C. Grayling, author of *The History of Philosophy* and *The God Argument*

I am completely down with the concept of contraduction. It fills a need. False pattern recognitions pose a real danger to our survival. Well done!

  – Ann Druyan, author (with Carl Sagan) of *Cosmos*, *Contact*, and *Demon Haunted World*

In a quiet and unassuming way, *Contraduction* is utterly brilliant. Every page has a thought so deep and unexpected that it stops you in your tracks, as you not only realize, "That's a different, really interesting way to think about the world, exactly the opposite of how I normally view things" but also, "And it is absolutely equally valid (and enriching) to adopt this opposite way of thinking." I loved this book.

– Stanford Professor of Biology Robert Sapolsky, author of
*Behave* and *Determined*

More and more I have come to believe that life is vastly more contingent than we realize, and that when we look at the past, we impose patterns of causation on it that may be backwards reasoning, or what Dan Barker calls contraduction in this incredibly insightful book. This is a valuable contribution to science, philosophy, and especially skepticism.

– Michael Shermer, author of *Conspiracy* and *The Believing Brain*

Entertaining, introspective, approachable. In *Contraduction*, Dan Barker instructs us on the foibles of subjective experience. In learning them we grow a deeper understanding of what we are as human beings.

– Hector Garcia, author of *Alpha God* and *Sex, Power, and Partisanship*

Dan Barker's *Contraduction* is a sharp new entry into the English lexicon. As a theist, I gladly assert that this is an accomplished and steel-manned argument. We may find that we have something to learn even from those we disagree with.

Dan Barker offers a very whimsical, yet thought-provoking perspective with *Contraduction*. I look forward to this new term being inducted into the dictionary in the near future!

*Contraduction* offers a new and fresh perspective on questioning our foundational beliefs. Barker's narrative is an amazing intellectual critique calling for a deeper and more humble engagement with the complexities of understanding. This is a must read for all thinkers!

*Contraduction* feels like a chat with a friend whose playful brilliance effortlessly exposes intellectual folly. Being disabused of one's errors never felt so good.

I love it when brilliant ideas are conveyed clearly and soundly. Dan Barker has provided a much-needed explication of a common fallacy that needs to be understood and rebutted. It is an engaging, enlightening, and insightful book.

With *Contradiction*, Dan Barker gives us a new word—and a new way of looking at things. I thoroughly enjoyed this! So much to think about—and it made me laugh. What else could I ask for?

– Kate Cohen, contributing columnist for the *Washington Post* and author of *We of Little Faith*

I love how Dan Barker offers us a new word to help us understand how to think rationally in a fun, simple way. I will never look at my reflection in the mirror the same!

– Bailey Harris, author of *My Name is Stardust*

Barker has really created something mega with this book. WOW, what an absolutely awesome mind bender contraductions are, while at the same time seeming very obvious. I give *Contraduction* 50 hell-yeahs! (outta 50).

– Zeke Piestrup, director of the films *Apocalypse Later* and *Satan's Guide to the Bible*

"Contraduction" the idea is such a wonderful, needed concept, and what a delight *Contraduction* the book is in explaining it! Dan Barker's writing is always so clear and insightful, and this book in particular shows his talents to full effect; it's simple, short and sweet—and yet contains worlds to think about…I love his new black-belt maneuver in intellectual ju-jitsu and the easy way it can change your whole universe just by turning your assumptions about the world inside-out.

– David Fitzgerald, author of *Nailed* and *The Complete Heretic's Guide to Western Religion* series.

*Contraduction* is a thought-provoking exposition of the hall of mirrors that we all must navigate. It provides a new term and perspective that can make us better thinkers.

– Matt Dillahunty, host of "The Line"

*Contraduction* is brilliantly conceived, thought-through and argued. Excellent job!

– Robert Richert, award-winning artist and author of *Open Wound* and *Apple Pie Atheist*

Dan Barker's approach reminds me of Douglas Adams' famous Intelligent Design analogy about the rain puddle that "fits me rather neatly." A simple shift of perspective can be invaluable in our understanding, and Dan's fresh angle gives us plenty to consider. Simply put, I've never read anything quite like *Contraduction*, and that's a good thing.

– Seth Andrews, author of *Deconverted: A Journey from Religion to Reason*

*Contraduction* offers delightful reading and presents a wise, reasonable voice with profound clarity that captivates and enlightens readers.

– Sanal Edamaruku, author and founder-president of Rationalist International

*Contraduction* is a delight and lights the way through complexity. Pound for pound, Dan Barker's best book.

– Ed Buckner, author (with Michael Buckner) of *In Freedom We Trust: An Atheist Guide to Religious Liberty*

# Contents

"All things being equal,
the simplest explanation tends to be the right one."
– William of Ockham

# Introduction

This book was conceived standing up.

In March 2022 I was in Orlando, at the invitation of the Central Florida Freethought Community,[1] to debate Adam Lloyd Johnson on the topic "Does God Exist?" As I was in the middle of my opening statement, standing before a large audience, a thought popped into my head.

In his opening statement a few minutes prior, Adam had raised the fine-tuning argument for a creator: The universe appears to be intelligently designed because if any one of the cosmic constants or forces were even slightly different, life would not be permissible. "Many thinkers have concluded," he said, "that the best explanation for this cause is some sort of a Supreme Being through abductive reasoning like an inference to the best explanation." (Abductive reasoning is a "best guess" or "most likely" kind of logic.)

---

[1] The Central Florida Freethought Community is a chapter of the Freedom From Religion Foundation, which co-sponsored that debate at FREEFLO, the Freethought Florida conference.

While walking up to the podium, as I thought about that word *abductive* some pieces came together, and I suddenly glimpsed what is wrong with the reasoning. It is backward. *Abduction* doesn't get you anywhere if you are pointed in the wrong direction. Groping for a way to put that amorphous idea into words, and thinking on my feet, I adlibbed: "I think we need another kind of word…called…*postductive* logic."

The audience did not seem impressed.[2]

After the debate, I pondered the meaning of that off-the-cuff remark. Was my epiphany an immaculate conception, or was it infertile nonsense? A couple of months later, as Annie Laurie and I were driving down the beautiful Pacific Coast Highway during a vacation, I was thinking about my prenatal conceptus of "backward" reasoning, about how we sometimes invert reality and flip our interpretation of what we observe. I noticed how perfectly the edge of the Pacific Ocean "matches" the shape of the California coastline. The western border of the North American continent appears to be a finely tuned puzzle piece that exactly fits the eastern edge of the ocean. But that is silly. Are there two connecting pieces, or are there simply two different ways of looking at a coastline? I realized then that *postduction* was the wrong word. I needed a prefix that means not "after" but "inverted." The concept conceived on one side of the continent was finally birthed as a new word on the other side.

---

[2]You can watch "DEBATE: Does God Exist? Dan Barker vs. Adam Lloyd Johnson":

https://www.youtube.com/watch?v=H32WynQMkc0 [bit.ly/3NSXHO4]

(A book about that debate called *Has God Been Found?* is in the works.)

When we got to Santa Barbara, we checked into the historic Cheshire Cat Inn and Cottages. I was eager to write down my thoughts, so the next morning (in the Tweedledum suite), now more firmly convinced that the abductive fine-tuning argument for the existence of God is just a toothy grin on an invisible cat, I got up early and started working on what I thought would be a short article called "Contraduction."

Over the months, the article grew as new illustrations came to mind. Readers of early drafts gave me useful suggestions. I submitted it to a number of magazines, but they told me (if they said anything at all) that it was too long. I sent it to a couple of book publishers, and they told me it was too short.

The lyricist Ira Gershwin was once asked, "What comes first, the music or the words?" He replied: "The contract."[3] When Hypatia Press offered me a contract to turn my long-form article into a short-form book, that changed everything. It gave me breathing room. (Or elbow room, as philosopher Daniel C. Dennett might put it.[4]) The article grew from a jingle to a song.[5]

In November 2023 I was in Oxford, England, to participate in another debate, and "fine tuning" came up again. This was my

---

[3] Mentioned in *Lyrics on Several Occasions*, by Ira Gershwin.

[4] *Elbow Room: The Varieties of Free Will Worth Wanting*.

[5] That is exactly what happened with the song "We've Only Just Begun," by Roger Nichols and Paul Williams, which began as a jingle for a bank commercial and later became a huge hit single by The Carpenters.

140th formal public debate (since 1985) and my second debate for the Oxford Union (since 2012). The topic this time was "This House Believes God is a Delusion." It was a three-against-three affair, with sociologist Phil Zuckerman and philosopher (and popular atheist podcaster) Alex O'Connor joining me to face off against Catholic Cardinal Peter Turkson, Hindu author Amish Tripathi, and Indarjit Singh, a Sikh who is a member of the British House of Lords. Richard Dawkins, author of *The God Delusion,* which prompted the topic of the debate, was in the audience.

Before we started, two very bright Oxford students gave opening statements. Chloe Davis, for the proposition, argued eloquently that theistic arguments can be replaced by science. David Logan, for the opposition, forcefully claimed that the appearance of "fine tuning" is evidence for an intelligent designer.[6]

We proponents decided on a group strategy: Phil laid the groundwork of our argument, Alex fleshed it out, and I went last to mop up with rebuttals to any arguments that might be raised by the other side. The only trouble was: none of the three invited opponents raised any arguments at all! They had simply given impassioned descriptions of their respective faiths. (Well, Tripathi did state that according to most Hindu teachings, we are all eventually gods, and if we are gods, God cannot be a delusion. I don't know if that counts as an argument.) It turned out that the only real substance I was left to rebut that night was Logan's well-crafted "fine tuning" argument. Since I had been working on this

---

[6]David Logan was charitable enough to read the manuscript for this book and provide insightful comments about my depiction of the fine-tuning argument in Chapter 10.

book, I was ready for that, although my remaining three minutes did not give me much time to flesh out a full rebuttal.[7]

*Contraduction* is my rebuttal to design arguments, especially the "fine tuning" logic. It also contains a possible refutation of the Kalam cosmological argument. As a developing argument that builds step-by-step, this book is intended to be read sequentially from beginning to end. You are welcome to jump ahead to a chapter that interests you, but if you do, you may miss groundwork that was laid earlier.

Ultimately, this book is not about the existence of God. It's about our brains. It's about the default self-reflexive assumptions we often make when looking at the world. It's about how we gaze into the mirror of reality and see ourselves looking back. Contraduction is an innocent fallacy of backward thinking that happens to all of us.

I'm not a professional philosopher or scientist. I'm a former ordained Christian minister who has had to think my way out of faith.[8] Now that I have discarded theology (a subject with no

---

[7]You can watch the entire debate at "DEBATE: This House Believes That God is a Delusion":
https://www.youtube.com/playlist?list=PLOAFgXcJkZ2xWv0tQcSmGS7uA-nkTsykt [bit.ly/3RS9hdo]
[8]You can read about my story in the books *Losing Faith In Faith: From Preacher to Atheist* and *Godless: How an Evangelical Preacher Became One of America's Leading Atheists.* You can also learn about more than 1,300 other clergy (so far)

object), I have found that philosophy can be fun. I hope you will enjoy the ride, and maybe chuckle along with me at the ways we sometimes fool ourselves, unknowingly reversing reality to fit our preconceptions. If there is any lesson in this book, I also need to learn it. Avoiding the easy path of automatically interpreting observations from the human point of view can be hard work. Like a continuity supervisor in a movie production, we can't just passively watch the film like the moviegoers do. We have to actively watch for mistakes. We must *assume* there will be mistakes. Otherwise, we may never see them, much less correct them to produce a life of continuity.

who have abandoned faith in the supernatural by visiting The Clergy Project at clergyproject.org.

# 1
# Backward

Why, sometimes I've believed as many as six impossible
things before breakfast.
– Lewis Carroll
*Alice in Wonderland*[9]

Have you ever been sitting in a train that's not moving when the
train next to you starts to move and you briefly think it is *you* who
is moving?

You got it backward.

Our brains sometimes unknowingly invert reality, and I think
these reversals occur more than we realize, and not just with moving vehicles. They can happen any time we make an assumption
based on our point of view. If we can recognize the backwardness
and flip things around, many perplexing questions in logic, philosophy, science, theology, and morality (and even in daily life)

---

[9]Spoken by the Queen to Alice.

might simply disappear. They don't need answers because they are not even questions. When we realize it is the other train that is moving, like Gilda Radner on "Saturday Night Live," we can say, "Never mind."

As far as I know, this backwardness does not have a name. What should we call it? Let me propose the word *Contraduction*.

Contraduction is an inversion of order. It can be a reversal of time, motion, position, causality, or relationship. Unrecognized, contraduction can sometimes lead to bad reasoning.

A silly illustration would be to wonder how so many rivers were made to flow along state borders. It must have been a huge civic project to divert those riverbeds to be exquisitely fine-tuned to the borders! But, of course, that is backward. The rivers came first.[10] Another silly example would be to marvel at how the shape of the human nose appears to be intelligently designed to support a pair of eyeglasses.[11]

Contraduction—like deduction, induction and abduction—contains the root *duct* from the Latin "to lead." *Deductive* (down-leading) reasoning produces conclusions from premises. (See example below.) *Inductive* (inward-leading) reasoning infers premises from observations. *Abductive* (away-leading) reasoning—sometimes called retroductive logic—is an inference to a possible explanation, producing not a strong conclusion but a best guess (More about abduction in Chapter 10).

---

[10] And notice that when the rivers veer from the borders, they head straight to the major cities.

[11] Which means people who wear contacts have an unnecessary protuberance in the middle of their faces.

Contraductive (opposite-leading) thinking, as I define it, is not a form of reasoning, good or bad. It is an informal fallacy that happens *before* the reasoning begins. It is what "mis-leads" your brain when the other train starts moving.

Not all contraductions are as frivolous as the idea that noses were created for eyeglasses. Some scientists, philosophers, and theologians claim that the universe appears to be "fine-tuned" for life. This leads to the abductive suggestion that there may have been a powerful intelligence behind the tuning. In Chapter 10, I will tell you how identifying a contraduction in one of the premises can nullify the conclusion (even the question) of the fine-tuning argument. (You can probably already see how, if you think about the moving train.)

A contraduction is a hidden fallacy. A backward-leading premise can sabotage logic without the reasoner knowing why. Look at this version of the Kalam cosmological argument that is sometimes used in debates about the existence of God:

Everything that begins to exist has a cause.
The universe began to exist.
Therefore, the universe had a cause.

That deductive conclusion is logically valid on its face. But is it sound? Are the premises true? Does everything that begins to exist have a cause? What does "begin to exist" mean? Is "the universe" (the set of all things) a *thing* itself that may or may not begin to exist? Did the universe in fact begin to exist? There are many questions we might ask about those premises, the answers to which may affirm or deny the conclusion. In Chapter 3, I will suggest that one of the premises in the Kalam argument may be contraductive.[12]

Does the sun rise? The idea that the sun rises and sets is an ancient powerful contraduction. Assuming that the earth is stationary, Ptolemy, in the second century, was forced to concoct a fantastic Rube-Goldberg-machine model of the universe involving improbable spheres within spheres to account for the apparent retrograde motion of the planets and the movement of the sun. The correction of the contraduction—the fact that it is *we* who are rising, not the sun—was not as easy as realizing that the other train is moving. Giordano Bruno was burned at the stake for the heresy (among others) of suggesting that the *earth* is moving, an idea contrary to established church teaching.[13] Even today a gaggle of flat-earthers and geocentrists defend the fallacy. And look at the rest of us: We continue to use the word *sunrise* while knowing it does not literally mean what it says. (What else would we call it? The *horizonset*?) Our language naturally reflects a human point of view and those conventions are usually harmless. But notice that it is the persistent human point of view that sets up the error. Bruno and Galileo, and Copernicus and Aristarchus before them, were able to question what seemed obvious to everyone else. They flipped the contraduction, resulting in the simpler and more elegant heliocentric model we now know is true.

---

[12]I discuss the Kalam cosmological argument in the chapter "Cosmological Kalamity" in my book *Godless*. *Kalam* is medieval Islamic scholasticism, which produced an early version of the cosmological argument.

[13]"The sun rises and the sun goes down, and hurries to the place where it rises." (Ecclesiastes 1:5) "From the rising of the sun to its setting, the name of the Lord is to be praised!" (Psalm 113:3)

We humans make a lot of mistakes. But a contraduction is not just any misinterpretation, bad guess, faulty reasoning, paradigm shift, confirmation bias, fallacy, or delusion. A contraduction, specifically, is a 180-degree mirroring of reality that can be blamed on a self-centric or self-selected point of view.

In the book *Killers of the Flower Moon* by David Grann, there is a photo of an Oklahoma homeowner and her servant. A woman is standing beside the door of a summer retreat. Seated next to her is a dark Osage woman. Some viewers of that photo might assume that the white woman is the homeowner, but it was actually the other way around. The Osage woman had become wealthy from oil rights and had hired the white woman as a servant. The automatic reverse relationship that some viewers of that photo might assume (by prior expectation) may be an implicit bias based on skin color or stature. An implicit bias—whether racist, classist, sexist, nationalist, or speciesist—is certainly self-centric. Whatever the reason, assuming the opposite relationship is contraductive.

Contraduction can swap cause and effect. For example, there is a strong correlation between smoking and depression. Hearing that fact, I immediately assumed that smoking can lead to depression and, if you stop smoking, you may be less depressed. Annie Laurie made the opposite assumption, that depression may lead to smoking as a form of self-medication. Why did I see it one way and not the other? Maybe you saw it like Annie Laurie, and maybe you are right. I may be presupposing a reverse causation. Either way, if there turns out to be a causal link, one of us is thinking contraductively.[14]

In his book *Conspiracy*, Michael Shermer notices a possible reverse causality: "There is a relationship between believing in conspiracies and being fearful, although it isn't apparent which way the causal arrow points."[15] For another example, some studies show that people who express gratitude are healthier.[16] But which way is it? Perhaps people who are less healthy are less likely to be thankful. Some studies show that older people who attend church are healthier than those who do not.[17] But if you are sick or homebound, you are naturally less likely to go to church! Some suggest that one of the causes of religion is death anxiety,[18] but maybe religion *causes* (or exacerbates) death anxiety. I do not know the answers to all of these questions, but whatever they happen to be, thinking about it the wrong way around is contraductive.

---

[14] The National Institute of Health says, "The relationship between smoking and depression remains controversial." According to "A cross-sectional study of smoking and depression among US adults: NHANES (2005–2018)," over the short term, Annie Laurie is right that smoking can alleviate depression, but over the long term "smoking increases the risk of depression."
https://www.ncbi.nlm.nih.gov/pmc/articles/PMC9922891/ [bit.ly/48dLvih]
[15] *Conspiracy: Why the Rational Believe the Irrational.*
[16] See "The Association between Gratitude and Depression: A Meta-Analysis": https://clinmedjournals.org/articles/ijda/international-journal-of-depression-and-anxiety-ijda-4-024.php [bit.ly/3HaWIoH]
[17] See "Attending Religious Services May Increase Lifespan": https://www.medicalnewstoday.com/articles/320581 [bit.ly/4lL3fjv]
[18] See "Death Anxiety, Religiosity and Culture: Implications for Therapeutic Process and Future Research": https://www.mdpi.com/2077-1444/12/1/61 [bit.ly/4aK9wzY]

That reminds me of the joke about the person who, when learning that most automobile accidents happen within a mile of home, moved to another city.[19]

Contraduction can sometimes lead to *post hoc* (after-the-fact) fallacies. Every day the rooster crows and then the sun rises. What a powerful rooster! This is obviously contraductive because it is not the crowing that causes the dawn. It is the dawn—that particular dawn or the millions of dawns in history that played a role in the evolution of roosters—that causes the crowing. Not all *post hoc* fallacies are contraductive. The groom caught a glimpse of the bride before the wedding and then their outdoor ceremony was washed out by a thunderstorm. This would only be contraductive if you were superstitious enough to believe that approaching storms cause grooms to take a peek at brides.

Since I am inventing the word, I get to define its usage. A contraduction is a fallacy, but the verb *contraduce* means simply "to flip around," either direction. This is similar to how *contradiction* can mean error while the verb *contradict* can go either way: if I contradict you, that doesn't necessarily mean you are wrong. To contraduce a relationship or causality is to reverse it, but in context—

---

[19]The humor in that joke might arise from a contraduction. Your home does not cause an increase in traffic hazards; the likelihood of an accident increases near your home because you spend most of your time driving there. You would experience the same thing wherever you decide to relocate. This joke would not work for a truck driver or traveling salesperson.

if we are noticing the fallacy—then *contraduce* can also be understood as "to correct" or "to overturn," like the phrase "overturning centuries of royal rule" means righting a wrong.

Rather than use the clunky phrase "Rube Goldberg machine" to portray an unnecessary and overly convoluted attempt to describe the appearance of a phenomenon that is the result of an unrecognized contraduction (like the Ptolemaic solar system), let's use *waldo*. The word *waldo* comes from the 1942 short story "Waldo" by science-fiction author Robert Heinlein.[20] In the story, Waldo Farthingwaite–Jones is a physical weakling who is intellectually brilliant. To overcome his limitations, he builds a fantastic remote-controlled device called the "Waldo F. Jones' Synchronous Reduplicating Pantograph" to make himself more powerful. The word *waldo* has come to mean a complicated and unnecessary explanation masking a simpler truth.

Waldos are messy. They are awkward. The word *awkward* originally meant "back-handed" or "turned the wrong way around," like a turtle on its back or a breech birth. If your explanation or argument doesn't feel right, doesn't always seem clear, doesn't fully click, or needs too many qualifications, it may be a waldo. There may be no way to fix it. You might be better off throwing it away. If you spot a waldo, look for the contraduction that created it, and if you find it, the problem might simply disappear. ("Oh. My train is *not* moving. Never mind.")

---

[20] *Three By Heinlein: The Puppet Masters, Waldo, and Magic, Inc.*

Sometimes we never realize the other train is moving. Like all innocent fallacies, contraductions are invisible. (I am going to assume the best about people. Contraductions are not necessarily the deliberate deceptions of conmen, magicians, or religious charlatans. They happen to all of us.) In the following chapters, I will offer some examples of how we might try to smoke out contraductions that we don't see, that we don't even imagine we don't see as we live our lives. I am not necessarily proposing anything definitive with these examples—you can be the judge of that— nor am I the first person to grapple with these concepts. Even if I am wrong about some of them, I am hoping these tentative thought experiments (*Gedankenexperimente,* as Einstein might have called them) will illustrate how we might try to identify and correct contraductory thinking.

# 2
# Time

The best evidence we have that time travel is not possible,
and never will be, is that we have not been invaded
by hordes of tourists from the future.
– Stephen Hawking
*Black Holes and Baby Universes and Other Essays*

In the 1970s and 1980s, I wrote some songs to accompany books
for children by Joy Berry. One song is about time.

### Time Never Stops
A tick and a tock and a tick and a tock,
Time travels by with each tick of the clock.
A second, a minute, an hour and a day,
A week and a month, then a year falls away.

Time travels by just the same for us all,
From winter to springtime, from summer to fall.
The sun always rises, the sun always drops.

The world keeps on spinning and time never stops.

Today turns to yesterday, first turns to last.
From future to present, from present to past.
The sun always rises, the sun always drops.
The world keeps on spinning and time never stops.[21]

Besides saying that the sun rises and drops—and, to my credit, correcting the contradiction with "The world keeps on spinning"—notice that I used the phrase "time travels by." I imagine, and you probably do too, that time is something that flows. I can picture the past and imagine the future, so it seems like I am at a spot on a continuum ("now") from which I can turn and look either direction: past and future events seem to be certain distances behind or ahead, flowing along a course or a river (Why do we never talk about looking sideways in time?[22]). I assume that there *is* a past and there *is* a future, because that is what it feels like from my perspective. My great-grandparents lived "back then" in the olden times, and my great-grandchildren will grow old in the faraway future, as if there were an increasing distance between now and then. (Why do we call them "olden times" when they were actually younger?). I can certainly describe time this way, but maybe my brain is just creating a model that I assume reflects reality, because, well, that is how it seems from my point of view. Just as the sun appears to rise, time appears to flow.

---

[21]"Time Never Stops" accompanies Joy Berry's Living Skills book *Every Kid's Guide to Using Time Wisely.* You can hear the song at:
https://youtube.com/watch?v=oi2O3KcGpiM
[22]Some physicists do talk about multidimensional time. Stephen Hawking's "imaginary time" can be rotated. He writes about this in his books *A Brief History of Time* and *The Universe in a Nutshell.*

The universal illusion is so powerful that some of our ancestors thought time was a god. When Annie Laurie and I visited the site of the original Olympic games in Greece, we saw the pedestals where statues of the god Kronos and his sister Rhea stood outside the entrance to the stadium in the eighth century BCE. Our tour guide told us that most scholars think the name Kronos meant "time" (hence chronology, chronic, and chronometer) and that Rhea comes from a word meaning "flow" (related to the root for "river," like Spanish *río*). So, Kronos and Rhea means "time flows." Or *tempus fugit*.

What if it is the other way around? What if it is not time that is flowing but *we* who are flowing? What if we are not in time, but time is in us? What if there is only now? What if there has never been a past and never will be a future, and what we experience as time passing is just the observation of material change in a timeless "now"?

That sounds weird. But what is time? Time is a dimension. "There is no difference between Time and any of the three dimensions of Space," wrote H. G. Wells, "except that our consciousness moves along it."[23] Notice that Wells did not say time moves; he said our consciousness moves. Albert Einstein (who was able to think weird, brilliant thoughts) helped to develop the concept of space-time, incorporating four dimensions. But is a dimension a *thing*? Where exactly is height? Is there a universal line somewhere that we can call width? It depends on your frame of reference, your point of view. As you grow from a toddler to an adult, are you traveling through height? You can arbitrarily draw

---

[23] *The Time Machine.*

a line anywhere and call it length or width or depth or height, and along that line you can set a zero point and measure distance by a specified unit and say, "My desk is 32 inches wide," or "That flagpole is ten meters high" or "Jupiter is 5.2 astronomical units from the Sun." The units are real, and the desk, flagpole and Jupiter are real, but those dimensions are just concepts, not things. We cannot talk about distance before establishing a relationship between two points.

Perhaps we can do the same with time. As there is no universal line we call height, neither is there a universal line we call time. Like the other dimensions, time is a concept; it "comes into existence" only when we need to measure. We establish a frame of reference and set a zero point. The units we use to measure time are not distances but movements. When someone says, "I am fifty years old," they mean they have traveled with the earth fifty times around the sun. They would not tell you their age by saying "I have journeyed 29 billion miles around the sun." Each revolution is one "tick" of the clock: one year. If you are ten minutes late to a meeting, the second hand has moved past six hundred ticks on a clock since the meeting started. The earth revolving and the clock ticking are not measuring time: they *are* time.

When you look at a star, the photons that hit your retina may have taken millions of years to reach you. That means you are seeing the star as it was then, not as it is now. From your point of view, you are looking into the past, like when you look at old photographs. (*Photograph* means "writing by light.") But from the photons' point of view, no time has passed at all. It is not as if the photons were patiently zipping along on an extended road trip across the vast expanse of space before colliding with your retina.

19

Photons "travel" at the speed of light (by definition) and, according to relativity, they do not age. For the photon, it is always "now." If you asked the photon, "How was your trip?" it would reply, "What trip?" When you look at a star, you are not looking *back* into history—you are looking *now* into history.

I am sometimes asked in debates if 2+2=4 is an objective truth that exists outside the mind (with the implication that there may be a transcendent realm of objective truth or immaterial reality). Regardless of how I might answer that question, Einstein showed us that 2+2=4 is not always true. At the speed of light, 1+1=1. So 2+2=2. When you shine a flashlight, the beam leaves you at the speed of light (in a vacuum). If you shine the flashlight forward from a speeding train, the light leaves you at the speed of light, but to an observer who is standing by the tracks, that light is also traveling at the speed of light, not the speed of light plus the speed of the train. Imagine you were shining the flashlight from a spaceship traveling at the speed of light (I mean theoretically; nothing with mass can travel the speed of light, but relativity is true at any speed, so the actual speed does not matter for the *Gedankenexperiment* or *thought experiment*). The light that leaves the light-speed flashlight at the speed of light would not be twice the speed of light to an outside observer. It would be simply the speed of light. Or 1+1=1. If our unit of measurement were half the speed of light, then 2+2=2. Imagine traveling at the speed of light and shining the flashlight *backward*. Would the light stop dead in space? No, it would travel away from you at the speed of light and also travel through space at the speed of light as seen by *any* observer. So 1-1=1. Not intuitive, but true.

In Einstein's famous e=mc² equation, the speed of light ($c$) is a constant. Energy (e) and mass (m) are variable. They can take different values, and they can change into each other, which is what is happening inside the stars that emit the photons that reach our eyes—but the speed of light stays the same. (Notice that *emit* spells *time* backward. Is that a contraduction?) Who would have thought that the world of physical objects and radiating energy we inhabit is anchored by *speed*? Speed is not a thing. Speed depends on time. If time is just a measure of change (which involves energy and mass), then maybe we can consider that what the change is measured *against* is $c$. From the light's point of view, there is no "speed." It is only we kinetic objects subject to entropy, from our point of view, who consider it to be speed. Maybe it is actually, contraductively, *non-c* that we call speed, and the inversion of that is what we call "the speed of light." The "now" that we constantly inhabit (with no past or future) is simply $c$. Light is "eternal," not in that it exists in an infinite stretch of endless time or that it never ceases to exist, but as a timeless constant "now."

If 1+1=1, then maybe past + future = now.

If that is true, *everything* is "now." Time is not flowing. Time may simply be the word we use to describe our impression of the changes that are happening around us and to us in a constant present. The appearance of "flow" (like the appearance that *our* train is moving), is the increase (or change) of entropy around us and in us (such as aging), and that is what we *mean* by time. The measuring is the time.

We are not growing older in time. Growing older is the definition of time.

21

I know this sounds wrong, because time is part of the equation we use to determine motion and change. An object moves through space a certain distance in a certain amount of time and we call that speed. Speed is d/t (distance divided by time). As time increases, speed decreases. But time, therefore, is just s/d (speed divided by distance), so time and speed are self-referential. The only real measurable item in that equation is distance: the amount of space objects may inhabit or pass through. The "passing through" is what we call time.

The contradiction comes from assuming that time is something we are *in*, rather than a dimension, which is a concept that is in us. You can't be "in" a dimension. You can certainly be "in" space-time, which is multidimensional, but that is just what the word *in* means. Since time is one-dimensional, you can't be in it. You might say you are *on* a dimension, but the line you are "on" only exists conceptually after you establish a frame of reference, so you are not on anything at all.[24] Except in your mind.

Suppose I hand you a group of photographs of a child's room that I have shuffled randomly. As you spread them out on the table, you see that in each photo the room is in various stages of disarray. In one photo, the room looks moderately neat. In another photo, toys, clothes, and pillows are scattered around the floor, the bed is unmade, candy wrappers litter the corners, the lamp has fallen over, and drawers are tilting out of the dresser. The images vary randomly from pristine to disaster. It should not

---

[24]If you are standing in line, that doesn't mean you are in a dimension. Mathematically, you are "on" the line. The line you are standing "in" is three dimensional. It is also four dimensional if the line is moving, and if it isn't, you are "in" distress.

be hard for you to rearrange those pictures into a temporal se-
quence, from neat to messy. As you scan across that line of photos,
you would be observing time passing.

How do you know to do that? You arranged those photos in
that order because you daily experience the second law of thermodynamics and have observed the increase of entropy in a closed
system. Especially if you are a parent.

But here is the nonintuitive point: When you look at that
spread of photographs, the concept of time passing in your head
is *no different* from any other "passage of time" you experience.
Scanning those photos, you are actually experiencing time "now"
just like you normally experience time "now" by remembering
what happened a minute ago or thirty years ago. Your entire life
is like that collection of photos, the arrangement of which con-
structs a concept we call "time." You are not seeing the events
occurring *in* time; the events occurring *are* time.

So my great-grandparents were not living "back then." They
were living "now." Certainly, to them it was "now," just like it is
to me. If time is not flowing, then the impossibility of time travel
is not based solely on the paradoxes (what if I "traveled" back and
killed my great-grandfather before he had children?) or technical
challenges (to "travel" to 1890s Oklahoma Indian Territory when
my great-grandmother gave birth to my grandfather would require me to actually travel through space to the point in our galaxy where Oklahoma was in 1895, more than half a trillion miles
away from here). Not to mention the moral issue of introducing
(or being introduced to) deadly novel pathogens. We can ignore
all of those practical considerations because time travel is simply
incoherent. We can't ask if time travel is possible or impossible

because time is not something you can travel at all. It is a measure of change in three dimensions, so there is no linear path you can take. The path is in your head. There is no place to go—you are already there. The idea that time might be traveled is *contraductory*. Like the appearance that the sun is rising, the idea of time travel is geocentric, or human-centric.

It's entertaining to imagine, but I don't know anyone who *really* thinks we could travel through time.[25] It is the stuff of science fiction and fantasy, like Alice stepping into the looking glass. If you truly think time travel might be possible, then you believe there is a future you might visit, which means the future is fixed. And that means that for your distant ancestors, *your* present (their future) was fixed. You are a determinist.[26] The only way to travel through time is to visit museums and archaeological sites, peer into space through telescopes, read history, look at photographs, watch old movies, listen to recorded music, and recall memories.

---

[25]Some experiments show that subatomic particles—like the tachyon—may sometimes travel backward in time (or faster than light), challenging the notion of time at the micro level. (See "An Extraordinary Particle Could Travel Back in Time, Scientists Say" at:
https://www.popularmechanics.com/science/a43012202/tachyon-particle-time-travel/ [bit.ly/3TOlGSg].) But in order for the huge amalgamation of atoms that comprise a biological organism like yourself to collectively travel backward in concert, every single one of the gazillions of subatomic particles that make up the trillions of vibrant cells in an organism like the human body would have to travel backward at the exact same instant, and continue doing so in a constantly functioning body for a noticeable period. In reality, those subatomic fluctuations cancel out and become meaningless at the macro level, similar to how the electrical fluctuations in each of your brain cells has no relevance to the thoughts you are thinking. Since entropy is a macro-level phenomenon, the actions of subatomic particles at the micro level have no relevance to how you and I experience time.
[26]See more on determinism and free will in Chapter 8.

"We all have our time machines," the actor Jeremy Irons says in the movie *The Time Machine*. "Those that take us back are memories. And those that carry us forward are dreams."[27]

Philosophers and scientists have been debating the nature of time for a long time. Presentism, eternalism, and B-theory also question our subjective experience. Einstein said, "The distinction between past, present and future is only a stubbornly persistent illusion."[28] But whatever time *is*, I'm simply suggesting that it doesn't *flow*. I'm not proposing time isn't real, any more than I would say the sun doesn't rise. We should continue using words like *sunrise* and *sunset* and *past* and *future* because they express meaningful concepts. Just as we can say—reversing a contradiction—that *we* are rising, not the sun, we can say *we* are flowing, not time.

---

[27]That quote was written by David Duncan and John Logan, screenwriters for the 2002 movie *The Time Machine* based on the novel by H. G. Wells. It was spoken by the character Übermorlock. The quote appears on the cover of a later edition of *The Time Machine*, but it is not documented that Wells ever said or wrote those words.

[28]Einstein said this in a letter he wrote to the grieving family of his close friend Michele Besso, who had just died. The broader context of that quote is: "Now he has departed from this strange world a little ahead of me. That signifies nothing. For those of us who believe in physics, the distinction between past, present and future is only a stubbornly persistent illusion." Einstein himself died a month later.

## Solstice Tribute

*O, shining star of solstice time,*
*Your radiant hours are few.*
*You turn and strike the New Year's chime –*
*We owe our lives to you.*
*These darkest days of winter,*
*We miss your warming rays;*
*But every year this hemisphere*
*Returns to brighter days.*

*Since olden days the human race*
*Has feared your warmth would die.*
*The evergreen is ever seen*
*As hope we will survive.*
*O, ancient drums stop beating,*
*And superstitions fall!*
*It's time for Reason's Greetings,*
*For peace, goodwill to all.*

– Dan Barker. May be sung to "O Little Town of Bethlehem"

# 3
# The Universe

Worlds on worlds are rolling ever
From creation to decay,
Like the bubbles on a river
Sparkling, bursting, borne away.
– Percy Bysshe Shelley
Poem, *Hellas*

There is an old joke that time is nature's way of keeping everything from happening at once. That's funny, but it might be the other way around. Everything happening is nature's way of keeping time. Time is not keeping anything from happening. Time has no power. As we saw in the previous chapter, *time* is a word we use to refer to the fact that things *are* happening. The room is getting messier.

Maybe we can apply this way of thinking to the universe itself. If we can invert the contradiction, perhaps we can see that the expanding universe is not a positive creation from nothing; it is a non-creation from everything. (Scientists describe the "beginning" of the universe as a singularity, a point of infinite mass and zero dimensions, but whatever it was, it was not *nothing*. We could just as well call it *everything*, which indeed it was at that point.) Flipping the image, the Big Bang may not be a construction. It may be an unraveling. A dying rather than a birth.

What happens when you heat a pot of water to boiling and then turn off the heat? The temperature does not drop immediately. It continues boiling for a while, cooling to a simmer, eventually reaching room temperature. As the pot cools, bubbles continue to appear and rise, getting smaller and slower as the heat dissipates. That is what appears to be happening with stars. In this analogy, the singularity at the "beginning" was the boiling point, and turning off the heat started the big cooling (aiming for the room temperature of absolute zero). When you look at the stars, you are seeing a partially cooled bubbling. Earth, next to a star that we call Sun, happens to be in one of the bubbles that is still "rising," still radiating energy during the cooling down, which gives us humans perched on a planet close to the shining star of hydrogen the impression, contraductively, that the flow of time emerges from an act of creation.[29] Looking at the big picture, however, we may be inside an act of un-creation. Bubbles are still rising, but the pot is cooling. From the perspective of brief organisms temporarily feeding off a localized reversal of the second law of thermodynamics—a negative entropy, or positive flow of

---

[29] Our Sun is in a magnetic "bubble" around the solar system called the heliosphere, created by the solar wind.

energy within the "bubble" of the solar system—life is emerging.[30] Evolution is happening. The child's room is getting neater. For a while.

If the Big Bang was really a Big Bust (as I call it), creating nothing (eventually) from something, then it was not a positive explosion. It seems like an emerging creation to us because as we ride the decay of winding down, we observe the appearance of temporary local bubbles in the process. Current cosmological models show that the universe is "open," that it will continue expanding and cooling until we reach an empty cold death billions of years in the future. The Big Bust is a massive dispersal of energy and a corresponding overall increase in entropy—the child's room is getting messier, not neater—and that increase in entropy is what we are calling "time."

Of course, our current understanding of cosmology is provisional in the absence of a quantum theory of gravity and may need to be adjusted in light of future discoveries. There is debate about the nature of the singularity. Is it just a theoretical mathematical concept (such as the definition of a point being zero-dimensional) or was there really a timeless point of infinite density and zero dimension 13.8 billion years ago? If that is true, then we shouldn't be asking how something came from nothing. We should be asking how nothing comes from something. Either way, the

---

[30]Informally, the second law of thermodynamics states that disorder increases in a closed system. More precisely, entropy increases. Entropy is the amount of energy in a closed system that is unavailable for work, meaning high entropy entails a uniform distribution of energy. (The messy room has high disorder. It takes work to put it back.) Mathematically, entropy is the result of dividing the average temperature of a system by its hottest point.

beginning would have been unruly. A state of utter nothingness, on the one hand, would not only lack matter, energy, space, and time, it would also lack laws; it would lack a law, for example, that says "nothing comes from nothing." On the other hand, the infinitely dense singularity, as opposed to utter nothingness, would be a completely chaotic state of unpredictability in which all natural laws break down, which means there would be no prohibition against the emergence of particles, space, and time. Either way, the beginning was lawless, and anything goes.[31]

Look at the Kalam cosmological argument again:

> Everything that begins to exist has a cause.
> The universe began to exist.
> Therefore, the universe had a cause.

That second premise—"The universe began to exist"—may be contraductive. It might be better stated: "The universe began *not* to exist." If that is true, as it stands, the Kalam logic fails.

You might object that this is just wordplay. You might think the Kalam argument could be fixed by changing the first premise to "Everything that begins to exist, or begins *not* to exist, has a cause." Beginning *not* to exist is still a beginning. We are in a universe that can be traced back to a start, whether we are expanding or shrinking, heating or cooling. Yes, but *beginning,* in that

---

[31] I discuss the concept of nothingness in greater detail in the chapter "Much Ado About" in my book, *Life Driven Purpose.*

sense, is just a concept, not an event, like when we talk about "the beginning of the twentieth century." What causes centuries to begin? Nothing does. The beginning of a century is just an arbitrary dating convention imposed by human thinking. Just because something had a beginning does not mean it had a cause. Since time itself came into existence at the Big Bust, there was nothing "before" that point, so we can't talk about it as if it were a point in time. (Neither can we talk about it as a point in space.) If we do talk about it as a "beginning," we are simply imposing a human dating convention on the universe.

With the pot of boiling water, the boiling indeed had a cause (the application of heat), and that was certainly a beginning. But the *stopping* of the boiling was not a cause: it was the *removal* of a cause. The singularity, whatever it was, fell apart when whatever it was that was keeping it together stopped keeping it together, and that is the *absence* of a cause. We can't use the Big Bust as an argument that the universe was caused.

The universe is getting colder. Cold is not a thing. Cold is the absence of heat, the absence of a cause. The universe is breaking down, not building up. We might also think of life itself not as the end result of some cosmic progressive creativity, but as a tiny bubble of temporary tenacious reversal during the inexorable universal decay. We are awake for a while—surprise!—but our natural state, contraductively, is to be asleep.

# 4
# Sleep

An endless sleep may close our eyes,
A sleep with neither dreams nor sighs.
– Robert G. Ingersoll
"Declaration of the Free"[32]

Here is another song I wrote for children:

**Sleep**
Sleep is the perfect way to end a perfect day.
Sleep can cure the blahs and blues.
Everybody needs it for health and rest.
Everybody needs to snooze.

There's no drowsy doubt about it, we cannot live without it.
Sleepy eyes were made to close.
Sleep is the perfect way to end a perfect day.

---

[32] The Works of Robert G. Ingersoll.

Everybody needs to doze.[33]

When I wrote "Everybody needs to doze," I was making an unspoken assumption. Can you spot it? We make the same assumption when we ask, "What is the purpose of sleep?" The idea that sleep has a purpose may be contraductory.

"Why do we sleep?" is a question asked from the point of view of being awake. If you are asleep, you would not ask (if you could), "What is the purpose of being awake?" It is assumed that wakefulness is the fully functioning state and that the temporary retiring into sleep needs to be explained. But what if it's the other way around? What if sleep is the default state of an organism and *wakefulness* is what needs to be explained?

We never ask if plants are sleeping. Trees are living organisms with a level of awareness, but since they are never conscious ("knowing that I am knowing"), it is meaningless to ask if they are asleep or awake. They simply live rooted (literally) in a state of "being alive." Other organisms are not rooted. We need to move around to find food, shelter, and mates and to escape threats. So we interrupt our sleep for a while—being awake an average of sixteen hours a day for humans, more for horses, less for cats—which can be seen as a *disruption* of the natural state.

Matthew Walker, professor of neuroscience and psychology at Berkeley and author of the book *Why We Sleep,* writes "Wakefulness essentially is low-level brain damage." We all know the feeling of sleep deprivation. Our brains function more poorly the longer we remain awake. Notice that I said, "the longer we

[33]"Sleep" accompanies Joy Berry's Survival Series book, *How To Go To Bed.* You can hear the song at youtube.com/watch?v=LO8XbuptEu0

remain awake," not "the less we sleep," inverting the contraduction.

I certainly enjoy being awake: exploring, learning, making music, reading, socializing, creating meaning. I could not have written this book in my sleep, I am pretty sure. But that all comes with a cost. Wakefulness is draining. Sleep is not something we add to our lives, like an activity we might select from a menu. It's an offer we can't refuse. Sleep is the default. It is not a waste of time. From sleep's point of view, being awake is a costly expenditure, a waste of sleep. Wakefulness is something we *take away* from sleep. How many times have you regretted being roused from a deep peaceful slumber? In the real estate market, houses or apartments are listed first by how many bedrooms they have. You know you are on your way to a good life if you can sleep comfortably and peacefully.

We sometimes call death The Big Sleep, as if that were a bad thing. But if you flip the perspective, it's not bad at all. When an old person approaches the end of life, it may be like they are coming to the end of a long busy day of wakefulness, happy but tired, wanting nothing more than hitting the pillow to drift back into the perfectly natural state.

"Death is not an event in life," wrote the philosopher Ludwig Wittgenstein. "[W]e do not live to experience death. If we take eternity to mean not infinite temporal duration but timelessness, then eternal life belongs to those who live in the present. Our life has no end in the way in which our visual field has no limits."[34] Wittgenstein was accused by some of dabbling into mysticism

---

[34] *Tractatus-philosophicus*, 1922.

when he said, "Eternal life belongs to those who live in the present." But that only seems mystical if you are thinking contraductively, as if "eternal life" indeed means "infinite temporal duration." What he did with "timelessness" in that sentence was reverse the contraduction. If we can't see that, we are stuck in a human point of view that requires waldos—fantastic "spiritual" explanations—to make sense of existence. Some versions of the hymn "Amazing Grace" contain the stanza: "When we've been there ten thousand years, bright shining as the sun, we've no less days to sing God's grace than when we'd first begun." But that only makes sense if you consider time or eternity to be an endless path stretching infinitely away. Eternal life, in that sense, is a contraduction. If there is only "now," the concept of an afterlife becomes incoherent and there is no need to construct a transcendent waldo realm with mansions and streets of gold where we will "not perish but have everlasting life." (Will there be bedrooms in those mansions?)

Here is the contraduction: Wakefulness is not modified by sleep; sleep is modified by wakefulness. Existence is not modified by nonexistence. We treasure being alive and awake because it is exceptional, a precious but temporary vacation from the natural state.

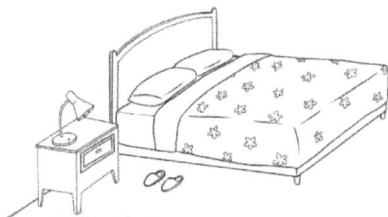

# 5
# Reflection

Now, if you'll only attend, Kitty, and not talk so much,
I'll tell you all my ideas about Looking-glass House.
First, there's the room you can see through the glass—
that's just the same as our drawing-room,
only the things go the other way.
– Lewis Carroll
*Through The Looking Glass:*
*And What Alice Found There*

We humans belong to one of the few species in which an individual can recognize itself in a mirror.[35] I think what we imagine we see in the mirror is a contradiction. If you raise your left hand, it looks like you are raising your right hand. If you part your hair on the left, it looks like you have parted it on the right. If you

---

[35]Some of the others include bottlenose dolphins, orca whales, Eurasian magpies, bonobos, chimpanzees, orangutans, gorillas, and chimpanzees.

hold up some text, the letters appear reversed and are hard to read.[36] In a mirror, left and right seem swapped, but are they really?

Despite the illusion, a mirror does not actually reverse left and right. If your right hand is to the east, the reflected right hand is still to the east. The left hand is still to the west. Our brains interpret it as reversed because we imagine that we are looking at another person "over there" looking back at us.

What a mirror really swaps is front to back. If you point your finger at yourself in the mirror, the finger in the reflection appears to be pointing back *toward* you. If you are pointing north, the reflection appears to be pointing south. *That* is what actually seems to occur in a mirror.[37] This is obvious if you hold your hand up. In reality you see the back of your hand, but in the mirror you see only the front.

In a mirror, width and depth appear reversed, but surprisingly, height does not. Have you noticed that the mirror does not swap top to bottom? Why not? This is true even if you are lying down. We sometimes see the word AMBULANCE in reverse capital letters on the front of the vehicle so that drivers looking in their rear-

---

[36]This is true unless the words have reflective symmetry, like "MOM" or "WOW" or "HAH" or "TOOT" or lower-case "tidbit." Another kind of symmetry is rotational. On New Year's Eve when I was eleven years old, I remember watching the year change from 1960 to 1961 and noticing that "1961" can be turned upside-down. (Can you think of the next year when that happens?) Ambigrams spell themselves upside-down. But these symmetries would only be (possibly) contradictive if the inverted word spelled a different word, like lower-case "mod" and "pow," if there were any meaning in that.

[37]The scientist Richard Feynman said something similar: "Richard Feynman Mirror":
https://www.youtube.com/watch?v=6tuxLY94LXw [bit.ly/3RMvFEX]

view mirrors can read it easily. But this only works if the word is horizontal. If AMBULANCE were spelled vertically, bottom-to-top, the reverse of what we might see on a tall narrow restaurant or theater sign, it would be worthless in a mirror.

The reason up and down do not flip is partly because top and bottom can be fixed relationships of an object. On the earth, you can describe "top" and "bottom" by referring to "up" and "down" as relative distances from the ground (or the planet's center of gravity). But you can't describe left and right in absolute terms. People often confuse left and right, but rarely top and bottom. Before you can know what an object's left or right side is, you first must establish a frame of reference: what is up and what is down. If gravity is the frame, this is easy: The point highest above the ground is "top" and the lowest is "bottom." But another frame of reference is the object itself. Many living creatures have a "top" and a "bottom," and this relationship does not change even if the body is rotated. Knowing that, it is possible to determine left and right perpendicular to a line that runs from top to bottom, no matter which way that line is oriented in space. (That's why top and bottom don't swap when you see yourself lying on your side in a mirror.) Humans are upright creatures with heads and feet, so top and bottom are easy to identify. But what is the top of a snake? What is the top of a cow? It might be the back of its head, not the "top" of its head. What is the top of a fish? It has a head and a tail, but since it is normally horizontal, unlike humans, we don't call its head the "top." We call it the front. What would a fish see in the mirror? Would it think its head and tail were reversed? If it had a sense of left/right, it might say "My left eye is now my right eye!" (It would more likely say, "Who is that other fish?")

But it is not just gravity or heads-and-tails. Suppose I show you a sphere or cube floating in space far away from a center of gravity. Or a blob or an object or creature for which we don't know its normal orientation. What is its right side and what is its left side? You can't know that if it is not marked "This End Up." Even if the sphere is spinning, you still have to pick a top and bottom. That is what we have arbitrarily done with maps of the earth. (Why shouldn't Europe be "down under"?) When a right-handed quarterback throws a football, the receiver sees it spinning counterclockwise (leftward on the top), but the quarterback sees it spinning away clockwise (rightward on the top). Which way is it? It's both. You can't answer that until you specify a point of view. Left and right, or east and west, are not real things. They are concepts dependent on other concepts.

After I wrote those paragraphs about top and bottom not appearing reversed, I realized that is not always true. It only applies if the mirror is vertical. I saw this when Annie Laurie and I were in the attic of La Pedrera,[38] an unconventional modernist building in Barcelona designed by Antoni Gaudí. "There are no straight lines in nature," Gaudí claimed, and except for the floors, that building has very few straight lines.[39] In order to produce an undulating rooftop, each of the hundreds of arched rafters is unique. Gaudí admitted he did not understand the math to produce those arches. He simply did it upside-down, as we saw in a display

---

[38]La Pedrera (stone, or quarry) is the informal name for the Casa Milà.

[39]This quote appears in the display in the attic of La Pedrera. I cannot find an original printed source. Gaudí's notes don't seem to contain the phrase.

illustrating one of his techniques. After attaching a flat piece of wood to the ceiling in his workshop, he hung a thin chain between two points to a certain "height," letting it drop in a natural parabolic shape. He attached many chains of different lengths to produce the wavy roof shape he wanted. Then he placed a mirror flat beneath it, and voilà, he looked *down* at the "upright" model. Engineers later confirmed that the construction is mathematically sound. When asked how he knew this, Gaudí replied that he got his ideas from nature.[40] While looking into a mirror on the floor, front-to-back becomes top-to-bottom, and top-to-bottom is swapped. The reverse happens when a mirror is attached to the ceiling. Notice that this does not change left and right.

Left and right have no mathematical definition. Like the clockwise/counterclockwise football, they are concepts that arise only after you establish a frame of reference. We might speculate that the person who first designed a clock face was right-handed

---

[40]This does not mean Gaudí was a philosophical naturalist. He was a devout Catholic who believed that God is the creator of all natural phenomena. His design of La Sagrada Familia cathedral, a few blocks away, is a testament to his soaring faith.

or wrote in a language that was read from left to right. If the ancient Israelites (whose script leads the other way) had designed the clock, would "clockwise" be the other direction?[41] Since left and right are concepts with no absolute definition, it is understandable that so many of us often mix them up, saying "right" when we mean "left," or vice versa.[42]

The way to contraduce the apparent mirror paradox is to un-reverse the image in your mind—not left to right, but front to back. When you look at a picture of yourself printed on a piece of paper, you see your right and left sides like another person sees you face-to-face, where left and right do *not* correspond in a direct line. But if you pick up the paper, turn it around and hold it up to the light and look through the back side, you will see your image like you see it in a mirror, where right and left do correspond. Now, instead of thinking of the paper as flipped around, think of *you* as having walked around to the other side, behind the front of the picture.

Do the same with a mirror. Instead of seeing your reflection as looking *back* at you, think of it as looking *forward* from you further along the path that the light would have taken if it had not bounced back. Think of the mirror as the flipped piece of paper you are viewing from the other side, looking *through* the image. Your face in the mirror is not looking *at* you; it is looking

---

[41]Clockwise probably has to do with how the shadows of a sundial move in the northern hemisphere. If sundials had originated in the southern hemisphere, clockwise would be the other direction. And maps would be upside-down.

[42]The Texas populist Jim Hightower quipped: "Two wrongs don't make a right, but three left turns do." (This quote was often printed in his newsletter, The Hightower Lowdown.)

*with* you. Away from you. Seeing it that way, right and left are aligned and you have corrected a contraduction.

# 6
# Life

We have this treasure in earthen vessels.
— 2 Corinthians 4:7

We don't have bodies. We are bodies.
— Christopher Hitchens[43]

I suggested in Chapter 4 that "spiritual" explanations are wal-dos.[44] The whole idea of spirit and soul may be a contraduction.

---

[43]"Christopher Hitchens vs. Rabbi David Wolpe: The Great God Debate."
March 3, 2010.
https://www.youtube.com/watch?v=2kZRAOXEFPI [bit.ly/48Fp8CM]
[44]I put the word "spiritual" in quotes because I don't think the word *spirit* has ever been defined in positive terms. It is always defined negatively as what it is not: immaterial, intangible, disembodied, noncorporeal, etc. Some have called spirit an "essence," but essence is not a thing or a property. Essence refers to the part(s) of a thing, anything at all, that are permanent, so it is nothing in particular. Whatever essence is, it is material, not "spiritual."

Many religions teach that our bodies are material receptacles for immaterial essences from an otherworldly domain. Some believe that a transcendent being implants eternal souls into our bodies at the moment of conception, and others believe humans became "living beings" when "the Lord God…breathed into our nostrils the breath of life" (Genesis 2:7). Even some nonreligious people imagine life is an ethereal essence that animates the body, a principle known as *vitalism*. It certainly seems that way. When a person dies, it appears that *something* has departed from its corpse. It no longer breathes or moves. Its heart no longer beats, and its brain stops functioning. When an animal dies, we call it meat. (Nonvegetarians do, at least.) If you eat steak, you probably don't think you are consuming a soul. So what is missing? Where did it go?

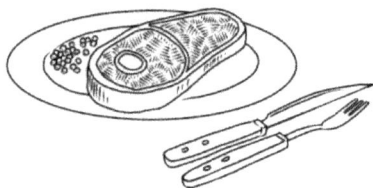

You would only ask that question if you think life is something that comes *into* a body from the outside. *That* is a contradiction. A living being is a functioning biological organism that radiates energy *out* of it. When the organism stops functioning—when it dies—nothing spooky has left it. The mechanisms that generate and maintain energy (measured in one way by body temperature) have broken down. A dead body gets cold. Like the pot of boiling water, it returns to room temperature. We biological organisms are like low-wattage stars that consume matter and radiate energy for a while before burning out.

The laptop I am using to write this book is also like a low-wattage star. It is not a biological organism, but it is responsive. While entering input and receiving output, I often communicate with it as if it were "alive" to some degree. (Have you ever talked to your computer?) When I turn it off, it returns to room temperature. I have been interacting with its functioning software, but now that it is shut down, its "life" is gone. Where did it go? I would only ask where it *goes* if I think it comes from outside itself, as if it had a soul hovering nearby waiting for me to resurrect its body so it can jump back in. (Fortunately, semi-conductors do not chemically break down quickly like brain cells or we could never restart our computers.) My laptop seems "alive," but only when it is functioning.

When a brain is functioning, we call it "mind." We have never observed a mind without a brain (or other physical hardware, such as a computer for artificial intelligence). This is because a function is not a thing. A function is a process *of* a thing. We have names for the functions or processes of other bodily organs, such as circulation for the heart and digestion for the stomach. When somebody dies, does anyone ask, "Where did their digestion go?" Just like the mind appears to be tethered to the cranium when the head moves through space, digestion appears shackled to the stomach. This is not because mind and digestion are tenants. It's the other way around. They are the work *of* an organ. Nobody would ask, "How does the sound of an airplane travel with the airplane?" Life is not a thing or essence that is inserted into the meat of a body; it is the sound of the entire body itself, the processes of the organs and the nervous system cooperating. When organs or nerves cease to function properly, we consider life to be compromised or diminished. When they all stop, we die. It follows that life cannot "live on" beyond the death of the body, even if time does flow. The idea of an immaterial soul is a waldo: an attempt to manipulate the puppet from a distance. To assume that life is an immaterial essence that *inhabits* a material body—"We have this treasure in earthen vessels"—is to commit the fallacy of contraduction. We don't have a life force—we *are* the life force.

Further, if life or a "soul" is implanted from the outside, then the fine-tuning argument for an intelligent designer becomes unnecessary. If life can simply be tucked into an object, then the creator could just as easily have injected a soul into a star or a rock without all the trouble of having to tune anything at all. Or, if the singularity at the Big Bust can be considered a *thing*, then "soul" could have been implanted into the very beginning even before the purported fine-tuning of the laws necessary for the emergence of the elements that provide the building blocks of matter and life. (See more on fine tuning in Chapter 10.) If theists respond that a soul may only enter a *biological* organism, they are merely mouthing the tautology that "Life may only enter something that is alive."

Of course, the words *soul* and *spirit* don't have to be used literally. A "spirited" horse is not possessed by a ghost. A "soulless" actor is not a zombie. Those words are used as poetic synonyms for energy, emotion, personality, even life itself. To think otherwise is contradictory.

46

# 7
# Morality

> "Love thy neighbor as thyself?"
> Hide that motto on the shelf!
> Let it lie there, keep it idle
> Especially if you're suicidal.
> – Yip Harburg
> "Do Unto Others" from *Rhymes for the Irreverent*

Another song I wrote for children deals with how to treat each other:

**Kindness and Respect**
Kindness and respect—
Qualities we need to learn, no doubt.
Kindness and respect—
That's what good manners are all about.

If you expect other people
To show their best manners to you,

You should respect other people
And treat them with kindness too.[45]

Those lyrics amount to a simple rephrasing of the Golden Rule, a principle that has appeared in most societies throughout history. Confucius said it around 500 BCE. The rabbi Hillel articulated it in the first century BCE. The New Testament Jesus (or his writers) repeated the idea a century later. Couched as a religious phrase, "Do unto others" carries a certain gravitas, as if it were a transcendent insight we would not have thought of on our own. But it's pretty basic. Children seem to know it instinctively (at least when *they* are treated badly). I prefer to call it the Bronze Principle because it is not really a rule, and because in spite of its obvious value, it leaves so much out of morality. There are better ways to say it. In her book *Elle the Humanist*, Elle Harris describes the Platinum Rule as: "Treat others as *they* would like to be treated." However it is phrased, this important principle seems to be a universal human precept, or law, that transcends history, culture, and religion.[46]

The word *transcend* has different meanings. It can be actual or conceptual. In theology, the supernatural world *transcends* the natural world as an actual realm above the mundane. While I am playing the piano, music theory *transcends* the notes I am playing

---

[45] The song "Kindness and Respect" accompanies Joy Berry's Living Skills book *Every Kid's Guide to Good Manners.* You can hear the song at:
https://youtube.com/watch?v=X-y4L.pyi-1c

[46] After reading a version of the manuscript of this book, the philosopher A. C. Grayling wrote to me: "In discussions of the Golden Rule, it was pointed out by GB Shaw that 'we should not do to others as we would have them do to us, because they might not like it.'" That is right. You might want to do unto others, but what if you have bad taste?

as a conceptual framework above the scales and chords. To mix one usage with another—to imagine, for example, that there is an actual realm of music theory beyond the physical world—is to equivocate.[47] Since the Golden Rule and other moral principles appear to transcend history and culture, we sometimes hear the claim by theists that since there is a moral law, there must be a moral lawgiver above and beyond humanity. That is an equivocation.

In *Mere Christianity*, C. S. Lewis proposes that since humans universally agree that there are actions we *ought* to do, or not do, we are admitting that we are governed by something outside of ourselves.

> "Consequently, this Rule of Right and Wrong, or Law of Human Nature, or whatever you call it, must somehow or other be a real thing...It begins to look as if we shall have to admit that there is more than one kind of reality; that, in this particular case, there is something above and beyond the ordinary facts of men's behaviour, and yet quite definitely real— a real law, which none of us made, but which we find pressing on us."[48]

Lewis suggests that there is "a Power behind the facts, a Director, a Guide" that he finds compatible with the god of Christianity who created the "Moral Law which He has put into our minds." When I was a minister, I used to preach that sermon, a message that resonates strongly with those who believe in a supernatural realm and don't know they are equivocating.

---

[47]A silly example of equivocation would be to say: God is love | Love is blind | Aunt Cora is blind | Therefore aunt Cora is God.

[48]*Mere Christianity*, Chapter 4, "What Lies Behind the Law."

But is that the only way to account for morality? Does it necessarily come from outside nature? I don't think so. I am not going to make a robust case for a natural moral philosophy here. I do that in my book *Mere Morality*. The whole question of morality can be summed up in one word: harm. If you are acting with the intention of minimizing overall harm, you are acting morally. And whatever harm is, it is natural. That means moral consequences can actually be measured and judged by reference to the real world, not by something "behind" it. This is a bottom-up principle, not a top-down law. Even if you think there is a better way to articulate a moral system, I think we can agree that as long as there exists at least one defensible naturalistic moral philosophy, there is no need to create a Man Behind the Curtain to guide our lives. We don't need stone tablets from a mountaintop to tell us there is something wrong with killing or stealing or lying. It is not too hard to figure out how we ought to live.

But where does the "ought" come from? Why *should* we act in non-harmful ways? I don't think "ought" comes from anywhere. Ought is not a thing. It is simply part of a conditional statement: *if* we wish to live in a world with less harm, *then* we ought to act in ways to minimize it.

There is much more to say about morality, but the point of this book is to see if we can spot the fallacy. The contraduction arises from viewing morality as top-down (commanded by a sovereign authority) rather than bottom-up (measured against the natural world). It puts the mirror on the floor. Of course, the mirror might be on the ceiling, and in that case we naturalists may be committing the fallacy. In any event, until there is good evidence or convincing reason to believe in a supernatural lawgiver, we rational agents can continue to lead ethical lives while viewing moral precepts as natural conclusions formed in natural brains.

But where did those brains come from? "How do rational agents come into existence in the first place?" asks Harvard professor of psychology Steven Pinker. "Unless you are talking about disembodied rational agents, they are products of evolution."[49] We are indeed natural organisms in a natural environment, but does that fact rule out creation? Are bottom-up evolution and top-down creation mutually exclusive? Some think not.

There may be a third option: theistic evolution. Maybe it is *both* top-down and bottom-up. There are some who believe in disembodied rational agency who nevertheless accept the fact of evolution. Theistic evolutionists have a compatibilist view: Creation and evolution are equally true. Perhaps an intelligent designer created the world in such a way that morality would indeed emerge organically, bottom-up, through natural selection, involving instinct, reason, and human law. That would make it merely *seem* that a transcendent lawgiver is unnecessary. If they are right, God ultimately gets the credit and we naturalists are the ones living under the contraductory illusion that we have discovered non-supernatural moral principles all by ourselves. But what difference does it make? "The invisible and the nonexistent look very much alike," philosopher Delos McKown wrote.[50] If God is going to so much trouble to conceal himself, what right do we have to try to flush him from his hiding place?[51]

---

[49]*Rationality*
[50]*The Mythmaker's Magic*
[51]See *The Hiddenness Argument*, by J. L. Schellenberg.

Prescriptive laws—human laws, which are different from the impersonal descriptive laws of nature—do not have a source. They have ancestors. We can see how human laws have evolved over time as societies learn to become less violent and more humane. We don't need a cosmic law. We have moral principles. Principles come first; laws follow. To think that morality even *needs* a source or a lawgiver is contraductory. Laws do not come *to* humans; they come *from* humans.

# 8
# Free Will

> Yes, I have free will. I have no choice but to have it.
> – Christopher Hitchens[52]

Maybe the idea of "free will" is contradictory. The ongoing debates over "free will" seem interminable and sometimes awkward, like trying to put together the pieces from two different puzzles while thinking it is just one puzzle. Perhaps that is because we are looking at the issue the wrong way around. You can see from the title of my book, *Free Will Explained: How Science and Philosophy Converge to Create a Beautiful Illusion,* that I consider "free will"

---

[52]I could not find a written source for this comment, but Hitchens did say this publicly many times, including in his 2010 Oxford debate with Scottish philosopher John Haldane: "We Don't Do God? Christopher Hitchens & John Haldane": https://www.youtube.com/watch?v=pflU-nnY4MA [bit.ly/3Hc6yXq] at 1:26:55. Hitchens may have been paraphrasing Isaac Bashevis Singer, who said: "You must believe in free will; there is no choice."

to be an illusion, which means I am a determinist. Determinists generally deny "free will" because we can't escape the fact that everything, including our brains and minds, is determined by the laws of nature. There is no wiggle room to sneak out of the laws of cause and effect. However, I differ slightly from some strict determinists who think "free will" is a pernicious delusion. I think it is actually a useful fiction, somewhat like *sunrise* and *future*. "Free will" is a reality in the same way the illusion of depth perception is a reality.[53] One helps us navigate the physical landscape, the other helps us navigate the moral landscape. Although illusions don't point to anything real, the illusions themselves are products of real brains. Since the illusion of "free will" appears to be universal, it would not be improper to ask whether it has an adaptive purpose. Maybe it doesn't. Perhaps it is just a by-product of consciousness, but since consciousness seems to be useful, we might just have to live with the illusion.[54]

You can see I have been putting "free will" in quotes, and that is because otherwise it might seem I think it is a real thing.

---

[53] Depth perception is an illusion because while the eyes send different images to the brain, the visual cortex combines them into a single image. You think you are seeing one image when you are really seeing two. Close one eye, and the stereo illusion disappears.

[54] The best explanation of consciousness I have read is by Daniel C. Dennett in his book *Consciousness Explained*, where he portrays consciousness as the "center of narrative gravity." The phrase "center of gravity" describes a measurable thing that does not actually exist. (What and where is the center of gravity of a donut?) Dennett, by the way, is considered a leading proponent of compatibilism, which he describes in his book *Elbow Room*. It is important to point out that compatibilists do not deny determinism, nor do they embrace any kind of spooky libertarian free will. Some people have called me a compatibilist, although I specifically say I am an acompatibilist. Just because someone finds the phrase "free will" to be useful does not mean they deny the scientific truth of determinism.

A better reason to put "free will" in quotes is because it has no universal definition. Scientists, philosophers, and theologians disagree with each other on what it means, not to mention whether we have it at all. Some consider "free will" to be a transcendent or supernatural property, usually called "libertarian free will" (not to be confused with political Libertarianism) that rises above or interferes with the deterministic laws of nature when we make a decision. That is indeed how it seems to most of us as we lead our daily lives: we *feel* free. Although we admit our limitations, few of us think we are *completely* constrained by forces outside of our power to make free choices. We don't live as if we were automatons. Others, usually called "compatibilists" (who claim to embrace both determinism and "free will"), consider it to be something like control or intention: the decision-making process or the choices of an agency. Others, like me, think "free will" is a convenient fiction (a social truth rather than a scientific truth) that can be used to justify moral and legal judgments: We demand that the person who committed the action be held responsible and accountable to the rest of us because (we assume) they should have known better and could have done otherwise. As individuals in a social species, we naturally project that figment of imagination back onto our personal selves. There are other definitions, and you may have your own. Even strict determinists, who deny "free will," need to define what it is they are denying—and even they do not agree. However, it seems the most common informal definition of "free will" is: the ability to have done otherwise. You pulled the trigger, but you didn't have to. Determinists say that since you pulled the trigger, you *had* to pull the trigger. Proponents of "free will" say no, you didn't.

The choices you make happen inside a brain that you did not create, and although you, as the agent who made the choices, are indeed socially, morally, and sometimes legally responsible for the consequences, your brain is just one tiny piece of an enormous array of gazillions of causes and effects (along with everyone and everything else) all determined by the laws of nature. You didn't decide to be born. You didn't choose how the DNA of your grandparents would randomly recombine to produce the particular arrangement of genes that shape your characteristics, appearance, physical strengths or weaknesses, preferences, desires, self-control, emotional temperament, moral inclinations, and mental aptitudes in math, music, language, art, memory, learning, reasoning, and so on. All of that was handed to you. It is also nurture, not just nature—you and your family, teachers and community have put some work into developing your character since you were born—but you have to admit that even the nurture, most of it, was outside of your control. And even the little bit of nurture that you do have some control over, such as your choice of peers or careers, is guided by the kind of person you happen to be in the first place.[55]

Stanford Professor of Biology and Neurology Robert Sapolsky, who denies free will, writes in his book *Determined*: "Once you work with the notion that every aspect of our behavior has deterministic, prior causes, you observe a behavior and can answer why it occurred." He concludes that "we are nothing more or less

---

[55]Steven Pinker lays this out nicely and comprehensively in his book *The Blank Slate*.

than the cumulative biological and environmental luck, over which we had no control, that has brought us to any moment."

There are many volumes written about all of this. The *Oxford Handbook of Free Will*, with almost 700 pages, hardly seems like a handbook. The philosophical and scientific arguments sometimes resemble theological disputes with proponents on either side strenuously defending their positions, as they should—as they are free to do. Perhaps the reason the debates are so intense is that this topic strikes at the very core of who we are. None of us wants to think our own personal thoughts and decisions are completely out of our control. If they are, then who are we?

It is a fact that we *feel* free, but feeling is not fact.

What do we even mean by the word *free*? The word *free* has different definitions and usages. It is often a fact that we *are* free, but freedom is not the same as "free will." Freedom is an external condition, while "free will" is an internal feeling. If I am not in a prison cell, I am free to walk outside regardless of how I feel about it. I am not free to run a three-minute mile, regardless of how I feel about it. (I am free to try, I suppose.) But this definition of *free* means "lacking obstacles or limitations," not "lacking the laws of nature." It doesn't matter if we feel free in the former sense. This distinction makes the word "free" in the phrase "free will" ambiguous or confusing, unless you consider the laws of nature to be an obstacle. (Some prefer to call it "free won't," meaning we have the ability to resist the deterministic laws that direct our choices.) And that probably is all the word *free* means in the phrase "free will": unencumbered by determinism. It's just a way of saying not predetermined.

There is much more to say about this, but let's cut to the point. As I mentioned in the Introduction, the messiness of a debate might be a clue that we are dealing with a waldo. To see if we might be harboring a contraduction, let's picture the illusion of "free will" as looking into a mirror. As discussed in Chapter 5, if you walk around to the other side of the paper to see that your image is looking not *at* you but *with* you, then you have reversed the illusion that the reflection is actually another person looking at you. (This is clearly an illusion because none of us seriously think our doppelgänger in the mirror is another individual with a mind of its own.) As we saw, mirrors reverse front to back, not right to left. In the "free will" context, think of front as the future and back as the past. The illusion of "free will" appears only when we look forward. When we look backward, the illusion disappears and the determinism is obvious. If we think the person in the mirror is looking back at us—or in the "free will" context, the person in our future is looking back at us—then it truly feels like we are free.

"Nothing is inevitable until it happens," wrote the historian A. J. P. Taylor.[56] But does "not inevitable" mean random or does it mean that we don't yet *know* how the cards will fall? Looking *forward* (imagining events before they unfold) is seeing through a

---

[56] *From the Boer War to the Cold War: Essays on Twentieth-Century Europe*. The full quote is: "'Inevitability' is a magic word with which to mesmerize the unwary. Only death is inevitable. Short of that, nothing is inevitable until it happens, and everything is inevitable once it has happened."

glass darkly; but looking *backward* (seeing how the cards were determined to fall) is seeing through the glass clearly, observing the world scientifically. We are sometimes good at predicting the future to a high degree of probability, but we can't examine the future. Within our minds, the future is subjective; outside our minds, the past is objective.

The illusion of "free will" comes from the fact that, while we evolved to try to anticipate the future—because those who are better at this have overall greater chances of survival—we cannot fully predict the future. If we could, we would not feel free. While attempting to anticipate the future, we hold options in our minds: perhaps this will happen, or that will happen, or if this occurs then that might follow, so I might do this, or do that, or choose this item over that item, and so on. From among the options we are juggling, we eventually make a decision (or perhaps decide *not* to decide) and that process, *while it is happening*, feels like freedom. The feeling of freedom arises from the state of uncertainty before we make the final decision. But if we knew the future, there would be no state of uncertainty, and no options to imagine and evaluate. We would simply do or think what we were determined to do or think.

If you know the future, you cannot have free will.

There is the contraduction. Looking *forward* to possible future decisions, it feels like we have free will. Looking *backward* to past actions, it is obvious we didn't.

←——————→

If it is true that "If you know the future, you cannot have free will," it follows that an omniscient creator who knows the future cannot have free will. If the future is fixed, that puts limits on the power of such a being. Prophecy and free will are incompatible. Prophecy is determinism. If gods do exist, they themselves might have a "feeling of free will" before making their own holy decisions, but their choices would also be predetermined by their own natures. They *must* be predetermined by their own natures, otherwise they are not gods—they would be no different from randomness and chaos. I don't know of any theists who imagine that their god makes whimsical decisions willy-nilly without reference to their character.

If God knows the future, God is not a free agent. God is a robot, not a personal being.

Some theists think they can get around this by claiming that God exists "outside of time." The creator and its creatures indeed have freedom, they claim, but since God created space, time, energy and matter, God's nature must be something "beyond" all of that, including time. (Does this follow? My children did not exist before I, and their mother, created them. Since my children are natural organisms, does that mean I must be a supernatural creator "beyond" their natural existence?) If you exist in a realm "beyond time," then you can indeed see it all at once, those theists suggest, because from that vantage point there is no before or after. The fact that a supernatural being can observe the results of freely chosen decisions from a timeless platform would not mean those decisions were not free when they happened. (When we dine out, Annie Laurie often predicts exactly what I will order for dessert. Does that mean I am not free? Sometimes, to protect the illusion of freedom, I will order something she did *not* predict, which proves nothing, except that she is not God.) If you are a being who exists "outside of time,"[57] the argument goes, you can accurately predict the actions of "free will" agents who remain morally responsible for their choices because they indeed really could have done otherwise. But only you know in advance how they will (or did) act.

But is that a satisfying argument? What could it possibly mean to exist "outside of time"? The word *exist* has many meanings, but if we are talking about a real being (instead of a concept), then to *exist* means to occupy space-time. (If you think *exist* means something other than that, you need to demonstrate how that works. Otherwise, *supernatural* is just a religious assertion with no measurable meaning.) Time is a measure of movement in space. *Outside* is a dimensional word that only makes sense *within* space-time. If you are outside of something, you are somewhere. Asking, "What is outside of time?" would be like asking, "What is outside of width?" I don't think theists understand what they are talking about when they say "outside of time." It's a handy, impressive-sounding phrase that seems to get God off the hook, but what does it mean? Until they come up with a coherent definition of how a *being* can *exist* who does not fall under the definitions of

---

[57]Those who believe in the god of the bible have to acknowledge that God does not act "outside of time." The Old and New Testaments describe God as creating, thinking, deciding, regretting, punishing, rewarding, changing his mind, burning cities, inflicting plagues, walking with Abraham, showing his backside to Moses, speaking to Job in a whirlwind, giving birth to a son, and so on. Those are all temporal actions.

*being* and *exist*, then to say that God exists outside of time is to say that God does not exist.

←•————————•→

Much has been written about "free will," dealing with the important issues of justice, moral accountability, blame, praise, consciousness, chaoticism, emergence, and so on. But I wonder if we are puzzled simply because we are looking through the back end of the telescope—through the glass darkly. Peering through that end, you will see only your reflected eye staring back at you. Just like we think time is flowing, or the sun is rising, or wakefulness is the default, or our face in the mirror is looking back at us, the idea of "free will" may simply be an artifact of how things appear from the human point of view. If we turn the telescope around and look through the eyepiece, we will see more than our own eyeballs. If we can get out of ourselves and simply observe—from the scientific point of view of an objective anthropologist rather than our own self-interest—the whole question of "free will" might simply disappear. It might not be a question at all. "Never mind." It's a contraduction.

Determinism is unavoidable. Even if you believe in a libertarian (transcendent or spiritual) free will, that itself would be determined by *something*—if not by known natural laws, then by some as-yet-undiscovered supernatural laws. I'm sure proponents of libertarian free will don't imagine it is all chaotic and random. We are all determinists.

However—and here is how I differ with some other determinists—I think we can continue to use the phrase "free will" just as we continue to say "sunrise," all the while admitting that what we are saying is not literally true. Let's consider ourselves *as if* we are free, like we continue to talk about the past and the future *as if* they exist. When a jury comes to a decision, we understand that their verdict is not truth: it is a statement that stands *as if* it were true, a "legal truth" or "social truth" that is not necessarily a scientific fact. Since we *Homo sapiens*, like all other species, are the result of the deterministic laws of nature, the same is true of our illusions. An illusion, like a verdict, is not nothing. While the objects of our illusions are not strictly *true*, they might sometimes be considered what Richard Dawkins calls the "poetry of reality."[58] Our often-beautiful conventions and inventions of thought and expression—such as metaphors and wordplay—can be useful guardrails as we navigate life on choppy seas.

Challenging this notion, a few strict determinists are like grammar police rapping knuckles: "You are saying it wrong!" Well, yes, sometimes we do say things wrong. But in everyday communication we can, if we choose, be charitable enough to admit that while a person's grammar may not always be perfect, they are indeed effectively communicating what they mean to say. Sometimes poetry arises from deliberately playing with grammar. Beautiful art is often the result of breaking rules. If I tell you I decided to compose a new song, will you chastise me with a reductionist lecture saying, "No, you didn't! The decision was the

---

[58] Richard Dawkins' audio/visual podcast "The Poetry of Reality" can be seen at https://thepoetryofreality.com/

result of your character and nature that was affected by evolved nerve cells inside your cranium that were created by recombinant DNA subject to the impersonal deterministic laws of cause and effect stretching back through your upbringing through your distant ancestors by natural selection all the way to the Big Bust!"? Of course not. You know exactly what I mean—that I am the proximate cause of the decision. You also know that *you* feel free. When you look into the eyes of your loved ones—even your pets—you don't view them as atomistic machines. When they choose to love you, you embrace their choice as freely given. When they choose to praise you, you feel something voluntary and warm, and that feeling is real. When you read a novel, you willingly suspend your disbelief and view the fictional characters "as if" they really exist. Can't you do the same with free will? Yes, yes, you are right, there is no free will. But to press the point can be overbearing.[59]

Contradiction inverts reality. The sun rises, but it doesn't. Time flows, but it doesn't. Your reflection looks back at you, but it doesn't. You have free will, but you don't.

---

[59]After reading this chapter, the philosopher A. C. Grayling (who is never overbearing) wrote to me: "We might not agree on Free Will. In Chapter 2 of my book *Philosophy and Life*, I give reasons why the concept is indispensable, at the very least an undischargeable assumption; and point out also that the basis of determinism—treating causality as an iron law—is questionable on Kantian grounds; it applies only to the phenomena, and one has to bear in mind that all the iron laws of current physics (even speed of light) have a reasonable chance of being subsumed as special cases of a more general and developed physics in the course of time (granting that time doesn't flow!)"

# 9
# Design

The universe that we observe has precisely the properties we should expect if there is, at bottom, no design, no purpose, no evil, no good, nothing but pitiless indifference.
– Richard Dawkins
*River Out of Eden: A Darwinian View of Life*

Before we get to the fine-tuning argument, we need to talk about design. There are a number of ways design arguments have been stated. Here is a common version:

> We have never observed design apart from a designer.
> The universe shows evidence of design.
> Therefore, the universe was made by a designer.

That conclusion is a stretch, of course, but it does amount to a plausible suggestion. It's a stretch partly because while science proceeds from what we do observe, design arguments proceed from what we do *not* observe: "We have never observed design apart from a designer," the argument goes. If we are allowed to induce a conclusion (rather than a premise) from what we *don't* observe, then we could just as well say:

We have never observed an effect without a natural cause.
The universe appears to be an effect.
Therefore, the universe had a natural cause.

Many theists would be uncomfortable with that conclusion, but this effect argument has the same logic as the design argument. I agree that that conclusion is not sound, but, like the design argument, it does place an option on the table. In this case, a nontheistic option. And if we must choose between them, which one should we start with: natural causation, which we know a lot about, or supernatural causation, which, so far, we know nothing about?

Before we talk about design itself, let's notice a blinding logical flaw in the design argument (as well as in my effect argument). It's a flaw that can occur in any argument that mentions "the universe," including the Kalam cosmological argument. You can't take a finding from within the universe (such as "We have never observed design without a designer" or "Everything that begins to exist has a cause") and then try to apply that finding to "the universe" as a whole, as if "the universe" were a thing that can inherit the properties of the elements. That is a category error. It improperly jumps up a logical level to create a meaningless conclusion. If all the members of an orchestra play in harmony with each other, does that mean that that orchestra is in harmony with all other orchestras? Since the elements in the set of even numbers are separated from their immediate neighbors by a distance of two, does that mean the set of even numbers is separated from the set of odd numbers by a distance of two? What could that possibly mean?[60]

Back to the point. If we are going to claim we have never observed design without a designer, we need to define terms. What does *design* mean? Is a snowflake designed? It certainly looks like it is. It is much more beautiful than the cut-out paper snowflakes deliberately designed by kindergarteners with blunted scissors. (More beautiful, except perhaps in the minds of their parents.) But the "design" of a snowflake does not arise from an intelligent mind. Do we imagine that tiny divine fingers carefully placed those molecules in artistic arrangement to create the beauty? The "design" of a snowflake can be explained by natural laws, by how atoms and water molecules naturally attract and connect. Are emeralds designed? Are the neat parallel ridges on a sand dune designed? Did a supernatural thumb or rake carefully score each of those evenly spaced lines like a Japanese sand garden? Those ridges on a sand dune are the result of wind, friction, and gravity. Like snowflakes, they were created not by intelligence but by the impersonal forces of nature.

I was walking along the coast of Lake Michigan in Door County, Wisconsin, in the early morning a few years ago, making footprints in the sand. As I was looking at the beach ahead of me, it struck me how smooth the gradient of sand was. Many of us

---

[60]This might be a reply to Russell's Paradox: "Should the set of all sets that do not include themselves include itself?" I don't think a set of sets is at the same logical level as a set, so the question is meaningless.

have seen that order, without paying much attention. Under the water, the rocks and pebbles are large and coarse. Further up the shore, they are smaller. From there, the sand particles get tinier and finer, nearly uniformly along the coast, displaying a simple elegance. Was it designed? Did a group of elves come out during the night to carefully sort each of those pebbles and grains in that precise arrangement? Or can we better explain the gradient by the fact that smaller particles (produced by erosion) get carried farther up the shore by the waves before dropping to the ground until the tiniest dust is deposited high enough to be blown away by the wind? When we can explain the "design" with natural laws (like hydraulic action and gravity), then we don't need to invent an intelligent artist.

If snowflakes and rubies are designed (by the laws of nature), then we have indeed observed design without a designer, and that knocks out the first premise in the design argument—"We have never observed design without a designer." It follows—at least by that line of reasoning—that the conclusion that "the universe was made by a designer" is unsound (unless that "designer" is simply the impersonal laws of nature).

Most creationists, therefore, must be claiming that "design" in the design argument refers to something more complex than simple natural phenomena. Perhaps they are talking about *determined* complexity, such as structures that serve biological purposes. But if you think about it, those structures were created by biological organisms that were themselves created by the simple laws of natural selection. Beaver dams, bird nests, wasp nests, bee hives, spider webs, chipmunk burrows and termite hills might appear to be "designed" by intelligence, but we can explain those structures as the result of survival instincts, not conscious design. Have you ever seen wasps or beavers begin their projects by analyzing blueprints and architectural drawings?

So what do proponents of intelligent design really mean by *design*? It can't simply be orderliness, because we can account for most order by the natural forces, like gravity. By *design* they must mean something more than sand dunes and chipmunk burrows. They must mean *functional* complexity, like machines—something that did not exist before human intelligence produced it. (Would there have been evidence of "design" on our planet before designing brains evolved?) In that case, *design*, to them, means "designed by intelligence." Indeed, that is how most dictionaries define design: something purposefully created by a thinking agent. Design, by that definition, is planned in advance, not naturally occurring without thought. This kind of design must include intention in its definition. And if that is true, then the first premise in the design argument—"We have never observed design without a designer"—reduces to the tautology: "We have never observed things that were designed by intelligence that were not designed by intelligence." And that, of course, begs the question. It smuggles intelligence into the premise that is aimed at concluding intelligence.

That's the problem. If you are *aiming* at an outcome, your options are limited. But if you are not aiming at anything, then what happens simply happens. Unplanned does not mean impossible. During my first semester at Azusa Pacific College in 1968, I was experimenting with paper airplanes in my dorm room. I tried various foldings. I tossed the planes at different angles and speeds. On one attempt, I held the little craft up near the ceiling and released it gently. The plane descended in a graceful helix completely around the room and disappeared deftly behind my feet into the slit of a bottom drawer that was slightly pulled out. Wow! I stood there relishing the moment. I didn't plan that, but I wished I had. I didn't attempt to repeat the feat. I knew that if I tried it a thousand more times, that exact trajectory would not happen again. If I had been *intending* that result before tossing the plane, I would have been very pleased with myself. I only enjoyed the surprising moment *after* it happened, imagining that I might have in fact intended it, while thinking, "What are the odds?!"

When you know the outcome *after* it happens, it can seem like it was intended. All of the other tosses of the paper airplane were just as likely as the one that made me smile, but I didn't say "Wow!" to any of those because they were uninteresting. The number of non-Wows is huge (maybe infinite?), but there is also a very large number of possible "Wows!" If the plane had landed on the floor upright, with its nose pointed to the ceiling, I would have said, "Wow!" If it had plopped into my coffee cup, or lodged perfectly into the heater vent, or poked into my textbook at the current lesson (reminding me to get back to my homework), I would have said, "Wow!" These would have been unintended random outcomes, yet I might have "seen" intention, after the fact.

The contradiction in the design arguments proposed by theists is similar to how the illusion of free will amounts to looking in a mirror. We look at nature and what do we see? Ourselves! Since *we* intelligent creatures design things that are orderly, when we see order in the universe, we superimpose something like our own aims upon that order. We look in the mirror and see a Grand Designer.

Creationists have it backward. Intelligent design did not create us. We created intelligent design.

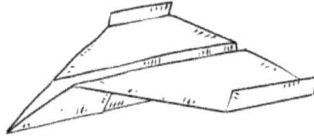

# 10
# Fine Tuning

Fish say, they have their Stream and Pond;
But is there anything Beyond?
This life cannot be All, they swear,
For how unpleasant, if it were!

. . .

But somewhere, beyond Space and Time,
Is wetter water, slimier slime!
And there (they trust) there swimmeth One
Who swam ere rivers were begun.
– Rupert Brooke
"Heaven"[61]

[61]From the 1914 poem "Heaven" by British poet Rupert Brooke, written the year before he died at the age of 27. I set that poem to music. A charming animated video of the song "Heaven," illustrated by Kati Treu, can be seen at https://www.youtube.com/watch?v=SOFA31t39mw [bit.ly/42cX1sL]

Now we come to the issue that prompted this book. The atheist Christopher Hitchens said: "At some point we are all asked what is the best argument you can come up with for the other side. I think every one of us picks the fine-tuning argument as the most intriguing."[62] The skeptic Michael Shermer agrees: "The fine-tuning problem…is the best argument that theists have for the existence of God."[63] I agree. The constants and parameters of the universe appear to be exquisitely fine-tuned for life. This suggests, to many, the possibility of a "fine tuner."

Scientists have identified about twenty parameters that determine the nature of our universe. These include the strengths and ratios of the natural forces (such as gravity, the electromagnetic force, and the weak and strong nuclear forces), the cosmological constant, and the rate of expansion since the Big Bust. "How surprising it is," wrote the agnostic physicist Steven Weinberg, "that the laws of nature and the initial conditions of the universe should allow for the existence of beings who could observe it. Life as we know it would be impossible if any one of several physical quantities had slightly different values."[64] If the chemistry of carbon were not what it is, biological evolution would be impossible. The theologian Alistair McGrath wrote: "Whereas it might be argued that nature creates its own fine-tuning, this can only be done if the primordial constituents of the universe are such that an evolutionary process can be initiated. The unique chemistry of

[62]Christopher Hitchens, speaking informally with Doug Wilson. https://www.youtube.com/watch?v=81P-jhiGM4U [bit.ly/3u6vU5V]
[63] The Believing Brain
[64]Weinberg, Steven, "Life in the Quantum Universe," Scientific American, October 1994.

carbon is the ultimate foundation of the capacity of nature to tune itself."[65]

"The existence of the universe as we know it rests upon a knife-edge of improbability," writes the theistic scientist Francis S. Collins.[66] The best way to explain this exquisite balance, some theists assert, is to suggest (abductively) that there may be an intelligent creator who tuned it all so that human life could emerge. "Even though it doesn't prove design, doesn't prove a designer," Hitchens continued, "you have to spend time thinking about it, working on it. It's not trivial." No, it isn't. At the end of his life, the philosopher Antony Flew was convinced by the appearance of fine tuning to abandon hard atheism. (Notably, Flew did not become a Christian. He called himself a deist, not a theist.[67])

The fine-tuning argument is a design argument (see previous chapter). It begins by observing that the physical values appear to be exactly tuned for life, and since we have never observed tuning without a tuner, the universe itself may have been tuned. By itself, as Hitchens noted, this doesn't prove the existence of a creator, but it does allow theologians to offer it as a hypothesis that may be compatible with science.

---

[65] *A Fine-Tuned Universe*

[66] *The Language of God*

[67] Deism, in short, is belief in an impersonal deity or creative force while theism is belief in a personal deity. Flew was not dogmatic about the fine-tuning argument. "I don't think it proves anything but that it is entirely reasonable for people who already have a belief in a creating God to regard this as confirming evidence." Interview on the UK's BBC "Belief" program, March 22, 2005. (By the way, some question whether the story of Flew's "conversion" during senility may have been exaggerated.)

In the debate over fine-tuning, theists and nontheists have offered several arguments to counter each other. Those waldo approaches, on both sides, are unnecessary. I think by now you can see why. We might be looking in a mirror. But first let me briefly describe those waldos before putting them aside.

The fine-tuning argument is based on probability. The likelihood of all those parameters balancing on the thin knife edge is so astronomically tiny that we can safely rule out coincidence, the argument goes. But in order to assess a probability, or likelihood, you need numbers. You need a denominator and a numerator. If I ask you to guess a number between one and a million, your chances of hitting the right answer are, well, one in a million. That is the number 1 (numerator) over the number 1,000,000 (denominator), written as 1/1,000,000. If I give you two guesses, that doubles the odds to 2/1,000,000. If we increase the numerator, the likelihood rises. If we increase the denominator, it drops. How do we know what those numbers are?

Picture a firing squad. You are blindfolded and tied to a stake to be executed by 100 expert sharpshooters. You hear the words, "Ready. Aim. Fire!" You hear the loud cracks of 100 rifles. But nothing happens. You are still alive. Most of us would insist that this surprising scenario cries out for a better explanation than, "Wow! I got lucky!" What are the odds that 100 rifles would all misfire simultaneously? That is theoretically possible but seems extremely unlikely. Did the shooters miss because they were *all* having a bad day? Maybe, but probably not. Did a mighty wind blow the bullets off course? That seems mighty dubious. Did the sharpshooters deliberately miss because they secretly love you? Were they making a political statement against the judicial system or the death penalty? The latter two possibilities seem more likely than random chance and would amount to an *intention* that you would continue living. If you could ask the shooters (or their leaders), perhaps that is what they might say.

You can probably think of other possibilities, but at the end of the day, some type of intention, or intelligent design, seems the least improbable. That's why Hitchens said fine tuning is the best argument theists can come up with. You won't have proof, but at least you have a good guess. What else can you do when you are blindfolded?

But then you remove the blindfold. You look around and are surprised to see what actually happened. There were 101 prisoners being executed that day. Nobody missed! You happen to be the one lucky prisoner, at least, who was not shot. Assuming the prior probability that none of the shooters ever misses, and that they all aimed at different prisoners, that changes the likelihood of your death from 100/1 to 100/101, which is now less than 100 percent. That means there was about a 99 percent chance of death, or almost 1 percent chance of survival for each prisoner. And there was a 100 percent chance that at least one of them would survive. That lucky survivor, whoever it is, would feel special. That is indeed how most of us feel who are alive on planet Earth.

Assuming that the cosmic parameters are variable and knowing that they must remain extremely close to their observed values in order for life to exist—that the sharpshooters never miss—

multiplying the probabilities of survival of all twenty or so parameters results in a monstrously huge denominator. Life, under that calculation, is vastly unlikely. We can't give exact numbers without knowing the ranges of allowable variance, but let's say it is something like $10^{50}$, or even $10^{100}$ (a googol). Let's call that gargantuan Large Number "LN." Assuming there is only one universe in which those values can vary randomly, we have an astronomically minuscule survival probability of 1/LN. That is not zero, but is close enough to be virtually impossible. That is the essence of the fine-tuning argument.

But what if the numerator can also vary? What if our universe is not the only prisoner being shot at? We might be living in a multiverse. If there are two universes, the probability of survival doubles (approximately) to 2/LN. As the numerator increases, so does the probability. We can't know the likelihood until we know both the denominator *and* the numerator. There might be LN universes, or $LN^2$ universes, meaning it would be a virtual miracle if there were *no* life anywhere. Life might be staggeringly rare, or it might be stupefyingly ordinary. (And if the numerator is infinite, you have already read this book.)

Another way to picture the odds is to imagine you are holding a box containing twenty different coins: a penny, nickel, dime, quarter, half-dollar, dollar, plus coins from other countries. I am holding a box with the same twenty coins. We both shake our boxes and then dump the coins on the table. What are the chances that we have the same arrangement of heads and tails? It's less than one in a million. You should not bet on it. But what if we do it a million times? Or what if there are a million people shaking boxes many times a day over many decades? In that case, you *would* bet there would be a match. Many matches. Our universe might be one of those "lucky" shakes, which is not so lucky at all, considering the large number.

I am not advocating for a multiverse here, although some scientists do.[68] A multiverse is not implausible. (For a theist to outright deny the possibility of multiple universes would be to limit God. Couldn't God create more than one universe if he wanted to?) The astrophysicist Victor Stenger once wrote me: "The multiverse is predicted by our best existing knowledge. It is in principle observable. As long as it remains plausible it serves to refute any argument that there had to be a creation and that the universe is fine-tuned." However, I admit, as Stenger did, that the multiverse *for now* is a waldo. "We should apply the rules of science and skepticism to the multiverse hypothesis as vigorously as we would any other," writes Michael Shermer in *The Believing Brain.*

For example, if we do live in a multiverse, that fact would prove too much. It would make it impossible to distinguish between coincidence and miracle (if miracles happen). What would a multiverse do to the concept of randomness? Suppose every time it thunders, we hear a voice saying, "I am the Lord thy God," or every time driftwood settles on the beach it spells, "Allah is great" in Arabic. Suppose prayers were always answered. I don't think any of us would say, "Well, we just happen to live in one of those universes where random accidental phenomena occur that happen to look like miracles but are just coincidence." We would want a real explanation. If there *were* a god, how could they

---

[68]Such as physicist Laura Mersini-Houghton, author of *Before the Big Bang*. A good overview of the scientists advocating or dismissing the multiverse (in its various forms) is found in Paul Halpern's book *The Allure of the Multiverse.*

convince us that we are not living in one of those universes where what appears to be a theophany is just a random occurrence? If there *were* real evidence for an intelligent designer, we would not recognize it.

Since we don't know what type of multiverse we might be in (if any), our speculations might lead to contraductive assumptions. If we are living in a simulated reality, for example, then maybe intelligent life was not created by the laws of physics; maybe the laws of physics were created by intelligent life. That creator could be a "god," or it could be highly evolved intelligences. It could also mean that even "God" himself, if he existed, would not know that *he* (or *she* or *they*) is not a simulation. The age-old question that even children ask, "Who made God?" would be unanswerable, maybe even unaskable, maybe even by God. "While multiple universes seem almost inevitable given our understanding of the Big Bang," the theoretical physicist Paul Davies writes, "using them to explain all existence is a dangerous, slippery slope, leading to apparently absurd conclusions."[69]

That may be true, but it does not mean that the idea of a multiverse has no value in an argument. It can counter one waldo with another waldo. A skeptic can say to a creationist: If you are going to posit a "best guess" of an intelligent designer, with no evidence, to explain the appearance of fine-tuning, then I will counter with a "best guess" of a multiverse with no evidence. If the waldo multiverse proves too much, the waldo designer proves too little. Like matter and antimatter, they cancel each other out.

---

[69]Paul Davies, quoted in "Is Our Universe a Fake?" by Robert Lawrence Kuhn (July 31, 2015). https://www.space.com/30124-is-our-universe-a-fake.html [bit.ly/48Suefq].

Like imaginary numbers (which are incoherent on their own), they can be used meaningfully in an equation if they cancel out. So far, neither of them proves anything. Someday, if the theoretical multiverse or the hypothetical intelligent designer is confirmed by observation, *then* we can ask whether either of them is responsible for the appearance of fine-tuning.

For now, let's set aside the multiverse. We don't need it. In his book *The Fallacy of Fine Tuning*, Victor Stenger points out that, although the probability of human life would indeed be very low if any of the currently known parameters were even slightly different, the probability of *some* kind of life is much higher than what many *Homo sapiens* theologians believe. Terrestrial life is not the only possibility. Stenger demonstrates that, if the parameters are like dials on a machine, and if you adjust more than one dial at a time, one in one direction and another in another direction, you can keep the entire cosmological system on a knife edge to be life-permitting in *some* form. "[A]s we allow all the masses to vary, not just one at a time, we will have plenty of parameter space for nuclei to form," Stenger writes. Like riding a bicycle, you can stay in balance with small corrections. "We see that when we allow more than one parameter to vary, fine-tuning is no longer evident. The parameter $\varepsilon$ is not fine-tuned to the range 0.006 to 0.008 but can take on a wide range of values if $\alpha$ is also allowed to vary."[70] If we think of life as broader than carbon-based

---

[70]The parameter $\varepsilon$ (epsilon) is what is called "nuclear efficiency": the fraction of the mass of helium that is greater than the mass of two protons and two neutrons. The parameter $\alpha$ (alpha) is the dimensionless "cosmic scale factor."

biological life, then the tuning does not have to be so fine. If the river had flowed differently, we would have a different border.

Sticking with our current values, there is still room to vary. In his article "Cosmology Without Design," physicist Lawrence Krauss shows that some of the constants are not so "fine-tuned" after all:

> "It is true that if the cosmological constant were much larger than it is, then life as we know it on earth would have been impossible; but if the energy of empty space were far smaller, even if zero, then galaxies would still be forming today, the universe proving even *more* conducive to life in the long run…A cosmological constant set to zero would have been a far better bet for a good designer."[71]

Proponents of fine-tuning rarely mention the fact that probability is useful only in context. "How likely would we think it was that there was a God, if we didn't know that the universe, the earth, or we ourselves exist?" asks Jordan Ellenberg in his book *How Not To Be Wrong: The Power of Mathematical Thinking.* Stenger points out that "fine-tuning" is meaningless if we have no basis for comparison:

> "It is claimed that the probability of the set of parameters that describe our universe occurring by natural processes is so incomprehensibly low that they must have been determined by some supernatural process. But nowhere do those who make this claim provide an actual comparison with the probability for the supernatural alternative, without which their

---

[71]"Cosmology Without Design." Available online at https://inference-review.com/article/cosmology-without-design [bit.ly/47zzOlF]

statements are worthless. Perhaps the probability is even smaller."[72]

Exactly. If the probability of life is 1/LN but the probability of a supernatural designer were, say, 1/LN$^2$, then it would be *much* more likely that life arose naturally, no matter how tiny the odds might seem to us. There is no way to know unless we can examine the creator and its environment.

◄━━━━━━━━►

When a raindrop hits your windshield as you are driving, are you impressed with the knife-edge precision of the trajectory? I'm sure you would not think: "What a great shot from such a distance!" Neither would you imagine *you* were on a fine-tuned course to intercept that raindrop. That is clearly contradictory. It's like a person shooting an arrow at the side of a barn, then drawing the target around the arrow after it hits. The apparent knife edge of fine tuning emerges *after* the event has happened, produced by observers *after* observers have evolved. (This is sometimes called the anthropic principle: the only universes that can be observed are those in which observers exist.)

In *A Short History of Humanity*, geneticist Johannes Krause and journalist Thomas Trappe write: "The hunter-gatherers' way of life was precisely attuned to millions of years of evolution, and it kept them in excellent health."[73] Notice that they do not say

---

[72] *The Fallacy of Fine Tuning*
[73] A Short History of Humanity: A New History of Old Europe

that the hunter-gatherers' environment was precisely attuned (fine-tuned) for their way of life. It was the other way around.

I have sometimes heard that one evidence for creation is the fact that the rhythm of plants perfectly fits the rhythm of the seasons. If seeds dropped from trees during the winter or the leaves fell off during the spring, they would die out. Creation Ministries International puts it this way:

> "All-or-nothing genetic cascades don't fit the claimed step-by-step evolution story, but rather fit with the Bible's account that plants were *designed* by a super-intelligent creator—God. He designed them to fit the *seasons* He made too (Genesis 1:14, 8:22; Deuteronomy 11:14). Autumn, and its colourful cascade of leaves, are no accident!"[74]

No, they are not an accident. The timing of the colorful cascade of leaves is a result of natural selection, triggered not by a designer but by the lessening of the amount of light as the planet tilts away from the sun. The contradictory creationists have it backward. The plants evolved not *for* the seasons, but *by* the seasons.

If the universe *was* fine tuned for life, why is most of it so hostile to our existence? The world could have been much friendlier. Why do we need to protect ourselves from the elements (needing shelter, heating or cooling, clothing, sunscreen, etc.), from an environment that was supposedly intelligently designed for us? Would a truly intelligent designer want to take credit for mosquitos? Why would anyone die from exposure? (Exposure to

---

[74]"Autumn leaves don't Fall (by accident)". https://creation.com/autumn-leaves-fall-by-design [bit.ly/3HnK7P8].

*what?*) Why can't we roam the vast cosmos? "The universe is trying to kill us," astrophysicist Neil DeGrasse Tyson often says.[75] Outside the little niche incubator in which an organism evolves—such as the thin skin of Earth's atmosphere or waters—nature is utterly hostile to life. And even within the niche, it can be dangerous. The universe appears to be exquisitely fine-tuned, not for life, but for death.

"The universe was not fine tuned for us," Stenger concludes. "We were fined tuned for the universe."[76]

←•——————•→

If there is an intelligent designer, the thoughts and intentions of that creator would appear to be the result of a mind that is itself balanced on a knife blade of perfection. Few theists would imagine their god asking, "How did my beautiful mind become so fine-tuned?" If the creator does not have to ask that question, why do we?

Using the logic of design arguments, we *could* answer that question:

> We have never observed intelligence that has not evolved.
> God is intelligent.
> Therefore, God evolved.

I doubt that creationists would agree with that conclusion.

---

[75]Tyson has said this numerous times. Here is one example: youtube.com/watch?v=Fw62e4SDHHo [bit.ly/3u2eHKZ]
[76]*The Fallacy of Fine Tuning*

The fine-tuning argument is not worthless, but it is based on the weakest kind of reasoning. An abductive argument has some value, but at the end of the day a guess is just a guess. In a criminal investigation, abduction leads to a list of suspects, or to a prime suspect. But suspects are real people. They can be interviewed. You can talk with family, friends, and coworkers, study their calendars and emails, receipts, and phone logs. You can examine security footage. If the investigators believe they have enough evidence to build a case, charges can be filed. You can't do any of that with the hypothetical "intelligent designer." Even if there *were* evidence for a creator, where is the evidence that they committed the crime?[77] A suspect is innocent until proven guilty. You can't simply say to the judge, "Here is our prime suspect, lock him up." You need to build a case and convince a jury beyond a reasonable doubt. Even then, defendants are sometimes wrongly imprisoned. At its most persuasive, the abductive logic of the fine-tuning argument cannot file any actual charges. It gets us only to a proposal that there *might* be a prime suspect. Those who make this argument have a lot of work to do before we make an arrest, much less arrive at a verdict.

---

[77]Calling creation a crime may not be hyperbole. Charles Darwin wrote: "I own that I cannot see as plainly as others do, and as I should wish to do, evidence of design and beneficence on all sides of us. There seems to me too much misery in the world. I cannot persuade myself that a beneficent and omnipotent God would have designedly created the Ichneumonidae with the express intention of their feeding within the living bodies of caterpillars, or that a cat should play with mice." Letter to Asa Gray, May 22, 1860.

But I wonder: Why does anything need to be tuned in the first place? Is that how creation works? Do theists believe the intelligent designer stumbled into a primordial soup of variables and decided to adjust them until everything came into precise focus for human life to exist? The very word *tuning* begs the question. When they say "fine-tuning," they are implying a "tuner" at the outset. As I explained earlier, that smuggles intelligence into the premise that is aimed at concluding intelligence. It's like asking, "If there is no God, who pops up the next Kleenex?" When you ask "who," you are forcing the answer to be a "who."

And what about angels? Many theists believe God created celestial beings which are, presumably, alive. Do those creatures dwell in an environment that was fine-tuned for *their* existence? If the supernatural realm has no constants to tune—natural or supernatural, whatever that means—then how can they live? (And what good are finely tuned wings in a realm with no material atmosphere?[78]) If spiritual life *does* require an environment that was fine-tuned, then wouldn't God himself (a spiritual being) be dependent on those same variables? If you believe angels and demons are living beings, then you don't believe it is necessary to tune anything at all in order to be alive.

←——————→

---

[78]Isaiah 6:2: "Above him stood the seraphim [angels]. Each had six wings: with two he covered his face, and with two he covered his feet, and with two he flew." Exodus 25:20: "The cherubim [angels] shall spread out their wings above, overshadowing the mercy seat with their wings."

Putting aside the waldos of a supernatural world or a natural multiverse does not mean there are no questions to be asked. Identifying the contraduction shifts the problem from cosmic to local. "What are the chances that the universe would perfectly fit us?" becomes "What are the chances that some kind of life would evolve to fit *this* universe?" We are looking not for an intelligent designer, but for an intelligent observer (using not a googol search but a galactic search). In that case, the odds are not astronomically low. They are planetarily low. Not all rivers flow along borders, and not all planets can potentially support life. Carl Sagan estimated that there are 300 million planets in our galaxy that could potentially support life. Since there are billions of galaxies, there must be quintillions of rocky planets that orbit a Sun-like star in a Goldilocks zone where water can exist as a liquid. Now, with the Webb telescope, we can *see* some of those planets. Even if the only kind of life we discover near us is bacterial or plantal, we will have confirmation that evolution is not unique to Earth. Gazillions of molecules in Earth's early oceans and lakes bombarded by gazillions of photons over a billion years produced at least one shake of the box that resulted in a simple replicator. One is all you need to get started. We have survived the firing squad and are free to evolve.

# 11
# Evolution

An ape, who from the zoo broke free,
Was cornered in the library
With Darwin tucked beneath one arm,
The Bible 'neath the other.
"I can't make up my mind," said he,
"Just who on earth I seem to be —
Am I my brother's keeper
Or am I my keeper's brother?"
– Yip Harburg
"We've Come a Long Way, Buddy"[79]

Charles Darwin's theory of evolution reversed a contradiction. Rather than seeing all species as fixed creations, with time flowing past them, Darwin saw that it is actually species that are flowing.

---

[79]From *Rhymes For the Irreverent.* Yip Harburg is the lyricist who wrote "Over The Rainbow," "It's Only a Paper Moon," and many endearing standards.

Life is bubbling like boiling water, not frozen in place. A species can exist for millions of years, but an individual within the species does not. Each of us dies, never to live again; but some of our genes can live on in our progeny. I doubt that Darwin saw time itself as a contraductive illusion, but he was able to reverse an order. The origin of species is bottom-up, not top-down—natural selection, not supernatural construction. Darwin was certainly concerned about how the church would react to the radical concept of evolution through natural selection, but perhaps another reason he delayed publication of *On the Origin of Species* for so long was the difficulty of convincing *himself* to reverse the powerful contradiction created by the human perspective.

In his groundbreaking 1976 book *The Selfish Gene*, Richard Dawkins contraduced that genes do not exist for the benefit of the organism.[80] It is the other way around. What this means, Dawkins said, is that natural selection "is best seen at the gene level…as a process of differential survival among genes, and therefore living organisms and their bodies are best seen as machines programmed by the genes to propagate those very same genes. In that sense we are gene machines."[81] Genes are not here for us; we are here for genes. If we reproduce, our genes live on. There actually *is* life after death, but it's not for you, and it's not eternal. Not able to recognize the contradiction, some critics thought *The Selfish Gene* was about genes for selfishness, or that genes are

[80] *The Selfish Gene* was listed as the most influential science book of all time in a 2017 poll by the Royal Society, ahead of Darwin's *On the Origin of Species* and Newton's *Principia Mathematica*.

[81] Richard Dawkins, PBS "Faith and Reason." pbs.org/faithandreason/transcript/dawk-body.html [to.pbs.org/3HLxuh7]

acting anthropomorphically selfishly. In *The Extended Phenotype*, Dawkins used the example of a Necker Cube (a simple outline drawing of the twelve edges of a cube) to demonstrate how we can view the same situation from a different perspective to describe things another way. People who can't make the switch are vulnerable to the fallacy of contraduction.

Evolution has been an established fact of biology for a long time, but some people, mostly creationists, continue to deny it for religious reasons. The Book of Genesis says, "In the beginning God created the heavens and the earth," and made everything, including humans and all animal life, in six days.[82] Today, of course, not all believers interpret those verses literally. Many of them, sometimes called theistic evolutionists, embrace the findings of science with no threat to their faith. Who are we, they claim, to dictate to God how he must create life? ("God, I demand that you do it poof—instantly!") The surprising wonder of nonintuitive natural selection might be exactly what the unpredictable actions of a creative deity would look like. Some believers think evolution *strengthens* their faith. (Of course, the messiness and brutality of predation and extinction during natural selection raises questions about the morality of a creator who would set up such a cruel system.)

I was not a theistic evolutionist. I was just ignorant. When I was an evangelical preacher, I believed evolution was wrong simply because it conflicts with the literal teachings of Genesis. That's as far as I thought about it. I don't remember taking a class

[82]This is another example that the bible portrays the creator as acting in time, contradicting the claim that God exists "outside of time," as discussed in chapter 8.

in biology in high school. (I do remember a physics class, so maybe that satisfied my science requirements.) I did take a class in botany at my Christian college, but it was mainly taxonomic. I understood that evolution involved change over time, but I had only a vague naive notion that completely inversed reality. I imagined evolution was a *thing*: a force, a positive progression, a developing drive, like when a baby grows to an adult. In my early thirties, I realized I didn't know much about what I was preaching against, so I decided to read about it. I picked up a few science books and magazines, thinking this would make my sermons more informed. (Shouldn't I have done that at the beginning?) As I was reading, I vividly remember how shocked and chastened I was to learn that I had been parading ignorance for so many years. "Oh," I thought, "so *that's* how evolution works. Interesting. That's not what I pictured at all. Wow. Natural selection is not a force. It is a filter. Wow! That is cool!"

Creationists, even theistic evolutionists, get it backward. It's not teleological. Species are not progressing to an intended end. Natural selection is subtractive, not additive.

An old hymn has the lyrics, "Thou art the potter, I am the clay."[83] But life did not arise like that. Evolution is more like sculpting in stone than modeling in clay. Yes, random mutations can "add" new traits to replicators, but the traits that produce variations that don't fit the environment (hence, "survival of the *fittest*") get whittled away—they don't survive, or they don't live long enough to reproduce, or they don't reproduce for other

---

[83]"Have Thine Own Way, Lord" (1907), lyrics by Adelaide A. Pollard, music by George C. Stebbins.

reasons, or they don't reproduce enough to compete with other species. Most mutations do not result in any survival advantage, and some are harmful, but over time, the very few that are "fit" are retained and the species gradually changes. During the Oxford debate I mentioned in the Introduction, Alex O'Connor said: "Survival of the fittest is the same thing as the death and destruction of the unfit." Natural selection is not a positive force. It is a pruning.[84]

Isn't this natural sculpting *more* wondrous than simplistic creation? We are who we are because of the natural environment in which we live. The planet does not fit us; we fit the planet. If we want to give a name to the sculptor, Mother Earth would be a better metaphor than Father God.

The shape of mountains might be a useful (if imperfect) analogy. The composer Johannes Brahms, whose music was often inspired by nature, liked to take long hikes in the foothills of the Alps.[85] During one of his week-long hikes, he sent a postcard to his friend Clara Schumann (wife of Robert Schumann), which contained the shape of the mountains he was viewing drawn on a musical staff. He turned that shape—where the rising and falling nodes hit the staff—into a melody, which became one of the themes of his First Symphony. Talk about creativity! But what

---

[84]Evolution is not necessarily progressive. Sometimes the organism ends up with less complexity, such as when parasites adapt to their hosts, shedding features they no longer need.

[85]*Johannes Brahms: A Biography* by Jan Swafford. Brahms was not religious. See my article "Brahms the Freethinker" in the May 2002 issue of Freethought Today:
https://ffrf.org/component/k2/item/18436-brahms-the-freethinker
[bit.ly/4aUysF1]

created the shape of the mountains themselves? After being thrust up by the tectonic forces of continental drift, the contours of those mountains were carved mainly by erosion. The softer material got washed or blown away first, leaving the harder material to erode last. (The Rocky Mountains runoff became the fertile fields of Kansas. The runoff from the Appalachians, which were originally much larger than the Rockies, became Florida.) I think, as a very rough analogy, we might see the "shape" of our own species as having been carved by the "erosion" of natural selection. The mutations that are "soft" (not fit for survival) get carried away while the genes that are "hard" (the fittest) remain to continue reproducing. It's an imperfect analogy, but you get my drift. The process is subtractive, not additive.

Maybe my personal misunderstanding of evolution was not representative of most Christians, but it does show how a contraduction might be reversed. In this case, our train is moving, and the other train is not (or not as fast). When I rejected evolution, I thought a species was fixed in place with nature swirling around it, but I now see it is the other way around. We species are swirling, developing, reacting, adapting, and evolving because we are a part of that very nature itself. We do not sit apart *from* nature; we a part *of* nature. Everything in nature that is not *you* sees you as part of the nature *they* are in. We are not just actors on a stage; we *are* the stage. There is no element in the universe that is more or less important than the elements that make up your body, and no part of your body is made up of anything that does not exist outside your body. You might see human-caused climate change, for example, as something we are doing to nature while we stand apart from it. In reality, we are inseparable from the nature we are affecting. In the long run, when nature changes, for whatever reason, we change with it. The waxing and waning of the Ice Ages happens slowly from the perspective of a single life, generation, or culture, but in the long run, the species that were affected by and survived those changes have been sculpted by those cooling and warming phases. That is evolution.

Human-caused climate change is certainly a huge threat to many species (not to mention individuals, families, and cities), and those that may survive and adjust to it will be said, after the fact, to have passed through a filter of natural selection. The climate has been changing for billions of years, with or without us. The universe does not care if we survive. We care. At least, I hope we care.

←———→

There is an old gospel song that says:

> This world is not my home. I'm just a passin' through.
> My treasures are laid up somewhere beyond the blue.
> The angels beckon me from heaven's open door
> And I can't feel at home in this world any more.

This view is backward. Just like we saw in Chapter 6 that it is contraductive to think that life (or "soul" or "spirit") is something from the outside that inhabits our bodies, it is equally contraductive to think that we are something from the outside that inhabits nature. We are not visitors from another world. We are the world.

Just as our image in the mirror is looking not *at* us, but *with* us, we can see that evolution is not happening *to* us, but *with* us.

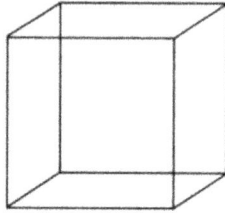

# 12
# Where's Waldo?

"Well! I've often seen a cat without a grin," thought Alice;
"but a grin without a cat!
It's the most curious thing I ever saw in all my life!"
– Lewis Carroll
*Alice in Wonderland*

So, what is the takeaway from this book? Contradiction may be an interesting concept, but what do we do with it? Why even care? We care because we need our premises to be true. And for that to happen, we need to observe from a perspective that is not tethered to our own point of view, whether personal, cultural, political, or religious. In other words, we need to do science. (Or as some might say: "We need to science!") Galileo didn't just muse about the universe. He didn't rely on personal opinion, revealed truth, or abductive reasoning when wondering whether the earth might be like the other planets. He was curious and cautious. He wanted to *see*, so he built a telescope. He was the first to describe the moons of Jupiter and the phases of Venus.

But in order for a telescope to work, we have to peer through the correct end—through the eyepiece. If we look through the awkward end, all we see is ourselves.

Each organism approaches the world first from its own point of view. That is natural. But valuing human life, as we should, we humans tend to rate human life as *the* value. Like an infant who thinks everything exists for "me, me, me!" we imagine that the universe was designed for "us, us, us!" Donald Johanson, the paleoanthropologist who discovered the "Lucy" fossil, thinks *Homo egocentricus* would be a more fit name than *Homo sapiens.* To think that *we* are the point—if there is a point—can set up many contradictions. Whichever train is moving, we always think ours is the important one.

We often don't see what is right in front of us.

If you were looking at one of those "Where's Waldo?" pictures without knowing it was a "Where's Waldo?" picture, you probably would not see Waldo. He would be right there in front of you, but if you were not actively trying to locate him, he would be effectively invisible, hiding in plain sight like an undercover officer. And even if you were told to look for Waldo, you have to know what Waldo looks like. It is only when you have been prompted and primed that you can begin your search. More than that, you have to *care* to find Waldo. As I mentioned in the Introduction, that is the attitude of a continuity supervisor in a movie production. After the film is edited, while everyone else is thinking about dialogue, performance, makeup, costumes, lighting, and audio, the continuity supervisor is deliberately look-ing for mistakes that the editor and producer missed, like a wine glass suddenly getting fuller, or a purse jumping to the other shoulder, or the clock on the wall moving back twenty minutes (now *that's* time travel!).

The purpose of this book is to prompt us to become our own continuity supervisors, actively searching for contradictions and the waldos that might be hiding within our own thinking. We have to *care* to look, otherwise our conclusions might be based on faulty premises or lazy habits, and we will waste time diving into a wonderland rabbit hole.

Now that you have a word for it, maybe you can spot a contra-diction of your own. When you complain about the traffic, do you consider that *you* are the traffic? If you are a composer, do you think harmony follows melody, or does melody follow har-mony? Is sexual intercourse penetration or envelopment? We might ask a similar question about colonization (and *that* cer-tainly depends on your point of view). Is Adam Smith's "invisible hand" of the economy a waldo? Is democracy an inversion of the divine right of kings? If we flipped top-down theology to bottom-up mythology, would the problem of the "hiddenness of God" that some theistic philosophers argue about vanish? (Does anyone fret over the hiddenness of leprechauns?) If time doesn't flow, was Kronos a waldo? Are all gods waldos? Did God create humans or did humans create God? (If God created humans, it seems there should be only one religion; but if it's the other way around, we should not be surprised to see that there are many religions, like there are many languages.)

In an article titled, appropriately, "The Sinner in the Mirror," the sociologist Phil Zuckerman uses the word *projection* to describe what might be an example of contraductive thinking. Projection, in psychology, is the assumption that what happens inside is coming from outside. In its positive usage, it is a basis of empathy. In its negative usage, it is a defense mechanism that projects your inner feelings onto another person, as if you were looking in a mirror. Sometimes when I describe my atheism to a believer, they will ask, "Why are you so angry?" This is not because I am angry; it is because what I have said makes *them* angry and they turn it around and project that anger onto *me*. Zuckerman points out that invading colonizers see "savages" when *they* are the savages. In America, "White Christian European settlers were projecting their own merciless urges, brutal motivations, and immoral actions onto their victims." White men called black men rapists when *they* were the rapists, treating enslaved females as sexual property. Mexican immigrants are called "lazy" when *they* do all the work the whites don't want to do. Believers call atheists "immoral" when they are feeling guilty for *their* immorality. Book burners think *they* are the ones being attacked.[86] Some women raised in purity culture who are sexually abused by "men of god"

---

[86]In *The Index of Prohibited Books*, Robin Vose writes: "Persecutors rarely see themselves as such, for they find ways to justify their actions as either fair or necessary, or both…understanding themselves to be the true victims of persecution…while painting their targeted enemies as genuine threats to be defended against." That paragraph is a good example of contraduction.

blame themselves for tempting those men.[87] An abusive husband says to his wife, "Why did you make me hit you?" And so on. Viewing a victim as a perpetrator is contraductive.

It's amazing what you might see once you are looking for it. After sending the final manuscript of this book to the editor, I spotted an important contradiction (and you will know the publishers were kind enough to add this paragraph). During a flight to Richmond, Virginia (the seat of the Confederacy), I picked up the book *Who's Black and Why?* at the airport and read about how white Europeans in the eighteenth century were coming up with the concept of race. Many of them, including prominent scientists and philosophers, thought black skin was a degeneration from the natural white skin of the human race. (Did you know that the word *Ethiopia*, from the Greek, means "burnt face"?) We now know it is the other way around. The editors Henry Louis Gates, Jr. and Andrew S. Curran write: "One marvels at how difficult it would be to explain in 1741: 1) that all hominids, including Homo Sapiens, originated in Africa and could only have been black-skinned; and 2) that white Europeans themselves were the fortuitous result of migration, mutation, and natural selection among vitamin D-starved bodies." Black skin and black/brown eyes represent the full pigmentation in the human genome. White skin and blue eyes are the real "degeneration." Paleness is the result of a mutation that causes full pigmentation to *fail*. This is somewhat like how green leaves lose their color and turn yellow or orange in the fall before they drop off. This is not to say that

---

[87]See, for example, the book *Disobedient Women: How a Small Group of Faithful Women Exposed Abuse, Brought Down Powerful Pastors, and Ignited an Evangelical Reckoning* by Sarah Stankorb.

fall colors are not beautiful or that white skin is truly "degenerative" (because it conferred a survival advantage in the north). It is simply to point out that the self-centered, xenophobic inventors of "race" (most of whom profited from the slave trade) got it backward.

In my book *Life Driven Purpose*, I invert the so-called Purpose Driven Life that some pastors preach. If you ask, "What is the purpose of life?" you are assuming life *has* a purpose. That is contradictory. If you think purpose is bestowed from above—from the orders of a commanding officer or the whip of a slave master—then you view yourself as a subservient vessel of someone else's goals. But if we flip the perspective, like looking into Gaudí's mirror on the floor, we can see that purpose is not top-down. It is bottom-up. To say there is no purpose *of* life is not to say there is no purpose *in* life. Purpose comes from trying to solve natural problems, and *you* are the one who decides what tasks to tackle. You don't need a master; *you* are the master. It is contraductory to ask, "If there is no God, what is the purpose of life?" That would be like asking, "If there is no Master, whose slave will I be?"

A few readers have told me they disagree with some of the ideas in this book. That is fine with me because none of them have disagreed with the concept of contraduction itself. I might be wrong about some particulars, but it is not the *what*; it is the *how* I am aiming at. When you look for a contradiction in your own field, don't just think outside the box. Turn the box around. Don't ask, "Where is Waldo?" Ask, "Where is the waldo?" Maybe we can discipline ourselves to observe the world unblinkered by the human point of view, and, as Wittgenstein said, "to think what cannot be thought."[88]

What do you think? Is the design argument dead now? That might depend on what you mean by *dead*. You can be killed or you can die of natural causes. You may or may not think I have murdered the design argument with sharp reasoning of my own, but that is not the point of this book. Contraduction shows (among other things) that the design argument has died a natural death. If the premise "The universe appears to be designed" is backward, the logic vanishes, the question passes away, and there is nothing to answer. If we think there is, we are projecting. We see a snowflake and think: "Something like me designed it." We imagine there is another person in the mirror gazing back at us—an intelligent designer!—but it's just us. We are simply looking at things turned the wrong way.

A woman called her husband to warn him that there was a report of a car going the wrong way on the interstate. "I know!" he replied. "But it's not just one. There are dozens of them!"

Proponents of the design argument are like the driver in that joke. He cries out for an explanation. He might imagine that those other drivers have quickly reversed course to flee from a threat, or that a detour sign was misplaced, or that they are conspiring to kill him! What he doesn't imagine is that *he* is the problem. The solution is not to plow headlong into those waldos. The

[88]*Major Works: Selected Philosophical Writings*

solution is to pull over, turn around, and head back to the natural world.

# Acknowledgments

Let's all give thanks where thanks is due,
Not to religion, not to a god,
But to the people who've made the world a better place
For me and you.[89]

The writing platform I use has an optional add-on AI feature that can help with composition. I was tempted to try it out, even if only to see what it thinks about this book. (Does AI think?) But I resisted the temptation. It would feel like cheating, or taking the lazy path. Perhaps someday I will warm to the idea of AI as an assistant, similar to how we use a thesaurus, grammar checker, or spell checker.

But for now, I am very happy with the UI (un-artificial intelligence) of *real* people, smart people who read various versions of the manuscript of this book and offered useful comments and criticisms. They made the book much more clear, accurate, and coherent. They sometimes saved me from embarrassment. These generous readers include Don Ardell, Dan T. Barker, Darrell

---

[89] "Let's All Give thanks" is a song I wrote for the Freedom From Religion Foundation's "Godless Gospel" project of secular lyrics in Gospel-music style, directed by former Gospel musician Andre Forbes. To hear the song, watch one of the concerts at https://youtube.com/watch?v=xHZ2TiLTyYY (starting at 15:00)

Barker, Ed Buckner, Aiden Culver, Mark Dann, David Fitzgerald, Anu Garg, Andrew Gaylor, Annie Laurie Gaylor, A.C. Grayling, Lou Immendorf, Miklos Jako, Ethan Johnson, Scott Knickelbine, Cheryl Kolbe, Lawrence Krauss, Aleta Ledendecker, Lisa Lee, John Loftus, David Logan, David G. McAfee, Adam Neiblum, Amit Pal, Jason Parker, Jonathan Pearce, Steven Phelps, Zeke Piestrup, John Quinn, Gricha Raether, Robert Richert, Will Robinson, George Rothdrake, Steve Salemson, Manel Salido, David Tamayo, Danial Tanvir, Marcos Telias, Mandisa Thomas, Amish Tripathi, John Widdicombe, Marian Wiggins, Peyton Williams, and David Williamson. And thank you, Shreyas Bharule, for the power cord you bought me in Mumbai after my luggage was mistakenly sent to Nairobi.

Special thanks to my talented friend, the Chilean artist Marcos Telias, for bringing the concepts to life.

·

# References

Barker, Dan. *Free Will Explained: How Science and Philosophy Converge to Create a Beautiful Illusion.* New York: Union Square & Co., 2018.

Barker, Dan. *Godless: How an Evangelical Preacher Became One of America's Leading Atheists.* Berkeley, California: Ulysses Press, 2008.

Barker, Dan. Life Driven Purpose: *How an Atheist Finds Meaning.* Foreword by Daniel C. Dennett. Durham, North Carolina: Pitchstone Publishing, 2015.

Barker, Dan. *Losing Faith In Faith: From Preacher to Atheist.* Madison, Wisconsin: Freedom From Religion Foundation,1992.

Barker, Dan. *Mere Morality.* Durham, North Carolina: Pitchstone Publishing, 2018.

Collins, Francis S. *The Language of God: A Scientist Presents Evidence for Belief.* New York: Free Press, 2006.

Dawkins, Richard. *The Extended Phenotype: The Long Reach of the Gene* (Oxford Landmark Science, paperback). Oxford: Oxford University Press, 2016.

Dawkins, Richard. *River Out of Eden: A Darwinian View of Life.* Reprint edition. New York: Basic Books, 1996.

Dawkins, Richard. *The Selfish Gene.* 40th Anniversary Edition (Oxford Landmark Science). Oxford: Oxford University Press, 2016.

Dennett, Daniel C. *Consciousness Explained.* New York: Back Bay Books, 1992.

Dennett, Daniel C. *Elbow Room: The Varieties of Free Will Worth Wanting.* (New edition) Cambridge, Massachusetts: Bradford Books (MIT Press), 2015.

Ellenberg, Jordan. *How Not to Be Wrong: The Power of Mathematical Thinking.* New York: Penguin Press, 2014.

Gates, Henry Louis, Jr., and Curran, Andrew S., editors. *Who's Black and Why? A Hidden Chapter from the Eighteenth-Century Invention of Race.* Cambridge, Massachusetts, Harvard University Press, 2022.

Gershwin, Ira. *Lyrics on Several Occasions.* Edited by John Guare. New York: Limelight Editions, 1997. The "contract" quote is mentioned on page 379.

Grann, David. *Killers of the Flower Moon: The Osage Murders and the Birth of the FBI.* New York: Doubleday, 2017.

Grayling, A. C. *Philosophy and Life: Exploring the Great Questions of How to Live.* New York: Viking, 2023.

Halpern, Paul. *The Allure of the Multiverse.* New York: Basic Books, 2024.

Harburg, Yip. *Rhymes for the Irreverent.* Madison, Wisconsin: FFRF, Inc. 2006/2024.

Harris, Elle. *Elle the Humanist.* Label Free Publishing, 2020.

Hawking, Steven. *Black Holes and Baby Universes and Other Essays.* Bantam, 1994

Heinlein, Robert A. *Three By Heinlein: The Puppet Masters, Waldo, and Magic, Inc.* (Book Club Edition). New York: Doubleday and Co., 1951.

Ingersoll, Robert G. *The Works of Robert G. Ingersoll*, Volume IV. New York: The Dresden Publishing Company, 1901.

Kane, Robert A., ed. *The Oxford Handbook of Free Will.* 2nd ed. Oxford: Oxford University Press, 2005.

Krause, Johannes and Trappe, Thomas. *A Short History of Humanity: A New History of Old Europe.* New York: Random House, 2021.

Krauss, Lawrence. "Cosmology Without Design," in *Inference-Review*, Volume 5, #3, September 2020.

Lewis, C. S. *Mere Christianity.* (1952), Chapter 4, "What Lies Behind the Law."

McGrath, Alister. *A Fine-Tuned Universe: The Quest for God in Science and Theology.* Louisville, Kentucky: Westminster John Knox Press, 2009.

McKown, Delos. *The Mythmaker's Magic.* Buffalo, New York: Prometheus Books, 1993.

Mersini-Houghton, Laura. *Before the Big Bang.* Boston: Mariner Books, 2022.

Pinker, Steven. *The Blank Slate: The Modern Denial of Human Nature*. New York: Penguin Random House, 2002

Pinker, Steven. *Rationality: What It Is, Why It Seems Scarce, Why It Matters*. New York: Viking, 2021

Rovelli, Carlo. *The Order of Time*. New York: Riverhead Books, 2018.

Sapolsky, Robert. *Determined: A Science of Life Without Free Will*. Penguin Press, 2023.

Schellenberg, J. L. *The Hiddenness Argument: Philosophy's New Challenge to Belief in God*. Oxford: Oxford University Press, 2015

Shermer, Michael. *Conspiracy: Why the Rational Believe the Irrational*. Baltimore: Johns Hopkins University Press, 2023.

Shermer, Michael. *The Believing Brain: From Ghosts and Gods to Politics and Conspiracies—How We Construct Beliefs and Reinforce them as Truths*. New York: Times Books, 2011.

Stankorb, Sarah. *Disobedient Women: How a Small Group of Faithful Women Exposed Abuse, Brought Down Powerful Pastors, and Ignited an Evangelical Reckoning*. Nashville: Worthy Books, 2023

Stenger, Victor. *The Fallacy of Fine Tuning: Why the Universe is Not Designed For Us*. Amherst, New York: Prometheus Books, 2011.

Swafford, Jan. *Johannes Brahms: A Biography*. New York: Vintage Books, 1999.

Taylor, A. J. P. *From the Boer War to the Cold War: Essays on Twentieth-Century Europe.* New York: Viking Adult, 1995.

Vose, Robin. *The Index of Prohibited Books: Four Centuries of Struggle Over Word and Image For the Greater Glory of God.* London: Reaktion Books, 2022.

Walker, Matthew. *Why We Sleep: Unlocking the Power of Sleep and Dreams.* New York: Scribner's, 2017.

Weinberg, Steven, "Life in the Quantum Universe." *Scientific American,* October 1994.

Wells, H. G. *The Time Machine,* 1895.

Wittgenstein, Ludwig. *Major Works.* New York: Harper Perrennial, 2009.

Zuckerman, Phil. "The Sinner in the Mirror: Why Atheists Are Stereotyped as Immoral." *Free Inquiry,* 43(2), February/March, 2023.

Dan Barker, a former Christian minister, is co-president of the Freedom From Religion Foundation with his wife Annie Laurie Gaylor. He is the co-host of Freethought Radio and Freethought Matters (TV) and a co-founder of The Clergy Project. His many books include *Godless: How an Evangelical Preacher Became One of America's Leading Atheists* and *Life Driven Purpose*.

www.ingramcontent.com/pod-product-compliance
Lightning Source LLC
Chambersburg PA
CBHW070812050426
42452CB00011B/2000